Content Marketing In A Week

Jane Heaton

Jane Heaton is a marketing consultant, content specialist and writer who helps people master the principles and practice of marketing and communications, from strategy to execution. A member of the CIM and a Chartered Marketer, Jane developed her business and marketing expertise in a small ad agency, in regional newspaper publishing and for brands such as Shell and Cable & Wireless – through hands-on experience and setting up and leading marketing teams. She started Jane Heaton Associates in 2000 to give businesses of all sizes access to expert marketing advice and skills – easily and cost effectively.

As marketing becomes more complex, Jane believes marketers must be able to confidently apply the essential core principles of marketing and think in a joined-up way in order to manage the growing choice of tools and tactics and deploy them successfully. Today she uses her wide-ranging experience and a blend of consultancy, mentoring, training and coaching to enable individuals and teams to create well-written, well-produced content as part of a clear, focused marketing strategy.

Find out more at www.janeheatonassociates.com, connect with Jane on LinkedIn at https://uk.linkedin.com/in/janeheaton and follow her on Twitter @janeheaton.

Content Marketing
In A Week

Jane Heaton

First published in Great Britain in 2016 by John Murray Learning

British Library Cataloguing in Publication Data: a catalogue record for this title is available from the British Library.

ISBN 9781473608252

eISBN 9781473608276

1

The publisher has used its best endeavours to ensure that any website addresses referred to in this book are correct and active at the time of going to press. However, the publisher and the author have no responsibility for the websites and can make no guarantee that a site will remain live or that the content will remain relevant, decent or appropriate.

The publisher has made every effort to mark as such all words which it believes to be trademarks. The publisher should also like to make it clear that the presence of a word in the book, whether marked or unmarked, in no way affects its legal status as a trademark.

Every reasonable effort has been made by the publisher to trace the copyright holders of material in this book. Any errors or omissions should be notified in writing to the publisher, who will endeavour to rectify the situation for any reprints and future editions.

Typeset by Cenveo® Publisher Services.

Printed and bound in Great Britain by CPI Group (UK) Ltd., Croydon, CR0 4YY.

John Murray Learning policy is to use papers that are natural, renewable and recyclable products and made from wood grown in sustainable forests. The logging and manufacturing processes are expected to conform to the environmental regulations of the country of origin.

Carmelite House

50 Victoria Embankment

London EC4 0DZ

www.hodder.co.uk

Contents

Introduction

Content marketing is one of today's growing marketing trends following fast on the heels of social media. Depending on what you read, it's either heralded as the latest and only way to market anything or it's a big fuss about nothing – because it's actually been around for years and it's just what most marketers do anyway, at least to some extent.

Using content in marketing is of course not new. It could be said that the first direct response advertising which used long copy to set out the benefits of a product or service represents an early form of content marketing. But in those days there was little choice when it came to getting your message out there. There was print advertising and PR and then along came radio and television.

The marketing landscape only changed significantly when the internet arrived and enabled us to do all sorts of exciting things – including publish our own content, easily and cost effectively. How much new content is published online every day is open to debate, but suffice to say it's a truly staggering amount. And that's changed the way we all look for, find and buy things – whether for personal use or in business.

Enter the opportunity for content marketing – marketing through creating and sharing content that potential customers find relevant, useful and valuable in order to attract, engage, convert and retain them. As such it's much more than simply producing a brochure and a set of product sheets to be used primarily by your sales team, or publishing the occasional newsletter or blog post.

It's a strategy that requires careful thought, clear objectives and goals, and a deep understanding of your audience. It requires you to reach out to them with well-planned and well-produced content – in all forms and formats, offline as well as online.

Although some companies may be able to adopt a predominantly content marketing approach, most integrate it with other marketing strategies that work well together and use content to enhance a range of other marketing activities.

In this book we take a joined-up look at content marketing, the key principles that underpin it, and what it takes to put it into practice in a consistent and fully formed way. And we provide a practical framework for planning it and executing it successfully – whatever the size of your business or your marketing team.

What we know as content marketing today may become the marketing norm for future generations. It takes time to deliver real results and you need to be willing to play the long game and build a relationship and trust with your audience over the long term. Adopting a content marketing approach is certainly not a short term, quick win tactic.

But the chances are it could make a big difference to the effectiveness of your marketing. Let's find out.

SUNDAY

Adopt a content marketing mindset

Today we set the scene for our work over the rest of the week and address some of the most commonly asked content marketing questions.

We look at what content marketing is and find out if it really is something new – or something we've been doing by default without realizing it.

Many businesses are focusing on delivering various forms of content to demonstrate their value and differentiate themselves from their competitors, enabled in recent years by developments in technology, the internet and social media.

But not everyone is doing it well. So, what are the key principles and characteristics of content marketing? What do we need to understand in order to be able to plan, manage and put it into practice successfully?

What is content marketing?

Content marketing is the process of marketing through creating and sharing content that potential customers find relevant, useful and valuable in order to attract, engage, convert and retain them.

You provide content that people actually want to receive – that informs, educates or entertains. Rather than marketing or sales interventions that are unwelcome – unwanted, irrelevant or intrusive.

It prepares the ground for a sale, helping you develop a trusted relationship with your prospect and moving them through your marketing and sales process.

At various points in that process you will employ well-crafted, call-to-action and conversion copy, but it will be appropriate and timely. Content marketing is not just advertising by another name – or an excuse to deploy gimmicky sales techniques to grab attention before delivering a hard-hitting 'buy me and buy me now' sales message.

The emphasis in content marketing is on genuinely helping your prospect to come to a well-informed buying decision, through a clear understanding of their issue or aspiration.

In many ways you are doing what the best-in-class, consultative sales person is doing during a face-to-face meeting, except that you are doing it with 'content'.

What do we mean by content?

The word 'content' is a bit of a catch-all term. The *New Oxford Dictionary of English* defines 'content' as 'the substance or material dealt with in a speech, literary work, etc. as distinct from its form or style'.

It is essentially *what* you are communicating. But you can present that 'what' – your core content – in different formats, in different places, using different methods of distribution and promotion.

Here's a simple example:

- Your 'what' might be an explanation of how your target audience could resolve a certain problem. For example, remove a red wine stain from a carpet.
- You could write this as a piece of 'how-to' text and publish it as a post on your company's blog.
- Or you could film a short video showing someone actually removing a red wine stain from a carpet and then publish the video on your company's blog and upload it to a video hosting platform such as YouTube or Vimeo.
- You could then draw your customers' attention to it by featuring it in your email newsletter or by sending out a specific email notification.

Content covers whatever you produce in text, image, audio, or video format wherever you publish or present it – on the web, in print, or in person.

Is content marketing new?

This example probably sounds familiar. So, is content marketing really new? Or is it something you've been doing for a long time already, but just not calling it 'content marketing'?

You may already be blogging, creating videos, producing newsletters, using social media and email marketing – plus doing a whole host of other content related activities.

So, is that content marketing?

The most likely answer is that although you may indeed be already using some form of content in your marketing, you may not be embracing content marketing in its fullest form.

If you are simply bolting some ad hoc content activities onto a 'traditional' marketing plan, you'll probably have some significant gaps.

The most likely ones are:

- Lack of a specific content marketing strategy that ties your content tactics together and integrates them with your overall marketing strategy.
- Lack of organization (a plan and tools) to create and publish content regularly to a consistent standard.
- Lack of measurement of content performance and return on investment.

This in itself requires a mindset shift for many marketers.

Although the *theory* of marketing strategy, planning and joined-up thinking is well known, in practice many businesses and marketing departments fall short under pressure to get on and just 'do' marketing – a way of working supported by the fact that, as marketers, we are often measured solely in terms of outputs.

Let's take the example of producing a customer newsletter.

We may be used to producing it four times a year. If we've been doing it for a while, chances are we've lost the connection with why we started the newsletter in the first place. It gets carried forward in the budget each year and we're primarily measured on simply getting it out on time each quarter. We may have some form of loose editorial planning in place but at some stage we get to the point of just wanting to get the thing finished. Once we've got the core article written, we're looking for fillers and scrambling to hit our deadline. We've become almost exclusively focused on the output, so we can tick that box and get on with our next task. And there's little desire or time to assess how well any one newsletter has performed – a difficult task made harder by the fact that we don't really know what we wanted it to achieve in the first place.

This is an example of using content (a collection of articles published in a newsletter) but it is not well executed content marketing.

 To be successful, content marketing has to be seen and treated as an end-to-end, joined-up process – driven by customer needs and a clear purpose.

Why an ad hoc approach to content is a bad idea

If you come to content marketing with a predominately 'doing' mindset, with just a glance at strategy and no real plan, you're in danger of becoming very busy writing and producing content and using up a lot of time and resources doing it with no clear idea of what you're getting in return.

In such a scenario getting ongoing support for your content marketing will be at best difficult – whether from your line manager, the management team, your fellow team members or others within your organization who you rely on as subject matter experts.

The seven key principles of content marketing

What then are the key principles and characteristics of content marketing that you have to understand and master in order to become the consummate practitioner?

1. Clearly understand the value you need to create for your audience

Your content is the means by which you will deliver value to your audience. Therefore you need to understand your prospects and customers in a deep and detailed way – to a far greater degree than you may currently be used to. You need to know all about your audience and what will make a real difference to their lives in relation to the products or services you are offering – in order to provide content that they will truly want and value.

2. Provide that value consistently, over the long term

Buying decisions are not usually made in an instant. Even a fairly low-cost product can have a wrapper of decision making around it. When you are in the washing powder aisle of the supermarket, your choice of brand and product is influenced by several factors – all unique to you, your values and beliefs as well economic factors and aesthetic preferences. And our choices are governed by habit. If you are providing a new eco-friendly laundry alternative you may be appealing to an innate desire to be 'green' (knocking on an open door) or have to work harder to educate and persuade someone to buy or switch, keep on buying and recommend your brand. This may take time and the building of rapport and trust – hence why we talk about the need to build relationships over the long term.

This is very different to most marketing campaigns. They tend to take place over months rather than years and have short-term sales goals. Content marketing, by its very nature, is all about playing the long game.

3. Measure results and ROI over the long term

In turn, this means that you can have no expectation of short-term financial pay back. This often presents difficulties in getting your business case for a content marketing approach or initiative adopted – unless your stakeholders and decision makers are all on board. The better news is that a lot of your content marketing efforts will be measurable – especially the part that takes place online as there is a wealth of web and social measurement tools available. The challenge however is to make sure you are setting up your content marketing so that a) you are able to measure it and b) you are selecting relevant, useful metrics to track. You want feedback that will allow you to test and improve performance of the specific content and channels you are deploying.

4. Be crystal clear on strategy and apply joined-up thinking

Content marketing is not the ad hoc execution of random content-based activities. It requires a strategy and plan that integrates with your overall marketing strategy and plan, and specific implementation plans for content creation, production, publishing, distribution, promotion and evaluation. Even when you have a simple strategy, these implementation plans are likely to be complex in the sheer number of schedules and activities to be integrated and mapped. So clear strategic thinking is crucial in order to provide direction and keep focused and on track – while being flexible and adaptable to marketplace changes.

5. Produce content regularly and consistently

Robert Rose, Chief Strategy Officer at the Content Marketing Institute, has referred to content as 'a show that never closes'. It requires commitment and resources to keep it going and maintain standards. It also means that you have to think more like a publisher or broadcaster than a seller of goods and services – and organize your team and workflow accordingly.

This inevitably shifts content from being a collection of marketing collateral to being more of a brand asset. You could be building up a store of valuable intellectual property. It's therefore important to consider where you host, publish and distribute your content and how you protect it. Make sure you own and are in control of the place where you keep and primarily display this asset (e.g. your own web domain) rather than relying on third party hosts (e.g. social media platforms) that can disappear or withdraw services – along with your content and followers – at any time.

6. Understand that distributing and promoting your content is as important as producing it

You can only do so much to get your content found by organic search. Even when you've mastered principles 1 to 5, you still need to build your audience through appropriate and timely distribution and promotion. Just writing and producing great content is not enough, you have to get it out there and, yes, shared and ideally talked about, used and acted on. This means bringing various marketing channels, tools and activities to bear and weaving them seamlessly into your content marketing strategy and plan. Things like email marketing, social media, partnering and even paid advertising.

7. Never neglect your internal communications

In order to get and keep support for your content marketing you are going to have to run and manage your own internal communications and PR campaign. This may involve helping to educate and win over the Board, the management team, your boss, your marketing team and other creatives, your agencies, and those people who you are going to be relying on as subject matter specialists.

When it comes to your marketing people, it's likely you're going to have to ask them to work differently, acquire new skills and take on new responsibilities. You may find yourself having to bring in new people with different skill sets. The old order may get shaken up a little or a lot. Be aware of the challenges and, as your content marketing evolves, ensure you are communicating effectively and involving and managing others appropriately.

Is content marketing a good strategy for every business?

As the concept of content marketing has gained momentum, more companies are producing more content – although not always as part of a well-rounded strategy.

Whenever something new or different comes along we, as marketing leaders or practitioners, ask ourselves, 'Is this something I should be considering?', 'Could this give us better results than our current approach?'

Ultimately, whether a content marketing approach will work for you depends on:

● the nature of your customer base and your customer decision-making processes
● how committed you are to properly planning and executing such an approach
● how willing and able you are to make changes.

In my experience, no broad generalizations hold true – such as that content marketing only works for B2B or B2C, or for those providing services, or producing products. You can use it effectively – to some degree – whatever your market, sector or offering.

That's not to say it's always easy to see how well it could work (or not) when you first start to consider it. In many cases, that's because we're all so used to looking at our business and our marketing in a certain way that's it hard to adjust our thinking. You need to start with a clean slate and no preconceived ideas – especially when it comes to tackling what your customers really want from you.

This may mean that you need to:

- work harder and devote more resources to understanding your customers
- be more creative and inventive in planning and designing content
- be more generous with the information, advice and value you provide as part of the process.

If you are involved in marketing a small business, then your content marketing landscape is going to be less complex than if you are a large, multinational enterprise.

Most companies who approach content marketing in a well thought-out way integrate it into their existing marketing plan alongside other marketing strategies.

Not everyone has the potential to become a fully-fledged brand publisher.

However, most businesses can benefit by thinking about and executing their content activities in a more professional way – looking at the content they are creating from their customers' perspective in order to provide something of genuine value rather than something that still looks like an advert or a sales pitch.

Summary

Today we've looked at what content marketing is and the core principles that underpin an effective content marketing approach. It's much more than simply adding a few content activities (like sending out a newsletter or writing the occasional blog post) into your existing set of marketing activities.

Content marketing is all about giving your customers real value – content that informs, educates or entertains. Content that they actually want and can use, that gives advice and answers questions. In this way it prepares the ground for a sale, attracting interest and keeping people engaged until such time as they are ready to buy. It's therefore a strategy that requires commitment over the long term.

Think for a moment about your own business. What content do you already produce as part of your marketing activities? Do you have scope to improve? Do you need to understand your prospects and customers better?

SUNDAY

MONDAY

TUESDAY

WEDNESDAY

THURSDAY

FRIDAY

SATURDAY

Briefly assess where you are at the moment and over the course of the week we'll see how you might develop, tailor and improve your content marketing approach.

Tomorrow we look at the different types of content formats and techniques at your disposal.

Fact-check

1. What is content marketing?
   a) A version of social media marketing ❏
   b) Marketing by providing and sharing content that people find useful and valuable ❏
   c) Another name for advertising ❏
   d) A form of email marketing ❏

2. What is content marketing especially good for?
   a) Annoying customers with unwanted direct mail ❏
   b) Delivering in-your-face 'buy me now' sales messages ❏
   c) Preparing the ground for a sale by developing a trusted relationship with your prospect ❏
   d) Distracting people from all the other things they have to do ❏

3. Is content marketing new?
   a) Absolutely – no one has ever thought of using content in marketing before ❏
   b) Definitely not – after all you've had a newsletter for years ❏
   c) No – it's exactly the same as email marketing ❏
   d) Using content in marketing is not new, but content marketing as a fully formed strategy has only come into its own in recent years ❏

4. When could you be said to have adopted a content marketing approach?
   a) When you throw a couple of blogs and few Tweets and Facebook posts together and call it content marketing ❏
   b) When you develop it as a well thought-out strategy within your marketing plan ❏
   c) When you bolt a few ad hoc content initiatives on to your existing marketing plan ❏
   d) When you just produce a couple of product sheets each year for your sales team ❏

5. How well do you need to know your audience?
   a) In a deep way so you know how your content can deliver value to them ❏
   b) Not that well, you'll just continue to guess what they want ❏
   c) Just enough to be able to make a sales pitch ❏
   d) It doesn't matter how well you know them, it won't make a difference to what you do ❏

6. Will content marketing always bring you a rapid return on investment?
a) Yes, it's a short-term, quick-win sales tactic ❏
b) It might, as long as you spend a lot of money on it in the first place ❏
c) No, because there's just no way to measure it ❏
d) No, you should expect to reap the rewards over the long term ❏

7. Why do you need a clear content marketing strategy?
a) You don't, having a strategy is completely unimportant ❏
b) It's essential in order to provide direction and keep your content marketing on track ❏
c) So you can then put it in your drawer and forget about it ❏
d) So you can feel smug in review meetings ❏

8. Why does thinking like a publisher help?
a) Because working for a newspaper or magazine seems more exciting than what you do ❏
b) It doesn't help at all because you're just here to sell stuff ❏
c) Because you need to take your commitment to content seriously and adopt a professional approach to publishing ❏
d) Because it will look good on your CV ❏

9. Is it enough just to create good content?
a) Yes, if you do that people will find it somehow ❏
b) Yes, as long as it's on your website Google will send you plenty of visitors ❏
c) No, you have to actively distribute and promote it across all your marketing channels ❏
d) All you have to do is mention it on social media when you first create it ❏

10. Should you tell anyone in-house about your content marketing?
a) No, no one within your organization will care what you're up to ❏
b) Yes, it's crucial you communicate in order to win support from your team, your managers and the Board ❏
c) Only if someone asks you ❏
d) No, you haven't got time to do that ❏

SUNDAY
MONDAY
TUESDAY
WEDNESDAY
THURSDAY
FRIDAY
SATURDAY

MONDAY

Understand the different types of content

We spend today taking a closer look at what we mean by 'content' and getting clear about the different content formats and options available to us.

We find content throughout our organizations – offline as well as online. I could fill this entire chapter with one long mega-list of different types of content, from white papers to blog posts, conference speeches to video clips.

But I'm not. Instead I'm going to walk you through the basic building blocks of text, image, audio and video, and the different techniques we can use to present our content in an attractive, audience-friendly way.

What I want you to learn is how to think about content in relation to your audience and decide what will work best for them and for you – rather than simply latching on to the latest trend.

SUNDAY

MONDAY

TUESDAY

WEDNESDAY

THURSDAY

FRIDAY

SATURDAY

Content scope

Over the past ten years, companies have been increasingly taking their marketing online, taking advantage of the opportunities opened up by the internet and developments such as social media.

As the term 'content marketing' has become more prevalent, you could be forgiven for thinking that's it just another form of internet marketing. But content marketing does not just take place online. Your customer's content journey spans the whole of your marketing process – both online and offline.

> **TIP** *What you are aiming for is to develop a seamless content experience for your audience that is consistent and congruent – wherever that audience finds you or interacts with your brand.*

The content items that you use to create this experience can be diverse and numerous or tightly focused and few in number – there is no right or wrong scenario.

Your content will include all your fundamental items, such as product and service descriptions and company information (because at some point in their journey that's likely to be what at least a proportion of your audience will be looking for).

But you'll also be creating new content that will take you beyond this descriptive, passive experience (even if it is already highly customer and benefits focused). You will be developing content that your audience can readily engage with and become involved in.

You'll be looking across your organization, thinking about content in a new way, assessing the role and value of the content items you already have, adding to or replacing some of those items and organizing and managing them in different ways.

At first sight, there can seem to be an overwhelming amount of content already in place and a mesmerizing array of new options.

Deciding what format to use

The one thing I never want you to do is to make a content decision that looks like this.

We must ... Add a blog to our website ... Create a knowledgebase ... Develop an elearning course ... Start a radio show or podcast series ... Develop a suite of videos ... Or any other content initiative you can think of ...

Because ... I've heard it's the 'latest' thing to do ... it seems to work well for [insert name of some well-known brand or competitor] ... we read about it in a book or just got back from a half-day course about a new content creation tool ... or any other similar, poorly thought out or knee jerk reason.

Even if (in fact, *especially* if) your boss, someone in sales, or your CEO suggests it – with no additional strategic rationale.

What ultimately determines the format and type of content you create are these two things:

● Whatever is going to best deliver the experience you want your audience to receive.
● Whatever is going to present your content to best effect and communicate with your audience most efficiently and effectively.

Not the latest trend nor shiny new tool nor a pitch from a product, service or training provider who's made no attempt to understand your business or your audience.

Becoming and remaining clear about the essential ways to categorize and think about content is therefore crucial in being able to successfully plan, organize and manage it. Especially when there seems to be a new flavour of the month ... well, every month.

Just because you hear that podcasting is the new blogging or that every website must have video, it doesn't mean it's right for you. The one thing I can guarantee is that by the time you read this there will be some new (or reinvented) technique that will be the latest 'in' thing. You'll see and hear lots of different people basically promoting and endorsing lots of different approaches and tools.

Keep in mind these simple, fundamental ways of thinking about content and avoid getting confused or distracted.

The basic building blocks – content formats

There are in fact only four basic content formats:

1 Text – words that you read
2 Images – still pictures that you see
3 Audio – words and sounds that you listen to
4 Video – moving pictures that you watch, with or without audio

Before we delve deeper into these, let's consider what each of them has to offer.

Each format gives your audience a different experience. That may sound a bit simplistic but it's easy to overlook this fundamental point when choosing the format for any one piece of content.

In many cases, you will also want to give a choice of formats. We each prefer to consume information in different ways. And our preferred choice can also change according to our circumstances.

- I may be drawn to listening to a half-hour podcast on a topic that interests me, but if I only have five minutes to get the key points, I will want to quickly scan the transcript instead.
- Audio may be great if I'm at home or in the car but impossible if I'm in the office or on the train without a headset or earphones.
- If I'm in research mode, I may want to print off pages.
- If I'm in learning mode, then I may have a preferred way of learning.
- And of course my choice of media and format can be influenced by the device I am using.

Text

Since man first put pen to paper, we've been reading the written word. Just because we've now got alternative media, it doesn't mean text based content is unwanted, boring or ineffective.

Nor should we be seduced or confused by research telling us that only short copy works these days because, thanks to the internet, our attention span is contracting and the competition for it is fierce. We're not talking about online copywriting here (although that will have a part to play in your overall content plan). We're talking about content that people actually want, that solves a problem: well-focused content that people want to engage with and learn from.

Therefore – when you are talking with the right people at the right time – well-written text-based content, whether short form (like blog posts) or long form (like white papers, in-depth case studies, or books) can a) still be the best primary choice and b) often an essential backup resource.

Images

Whether or not you think a picture is worth a thousand words, images can do an excellent job of supporting your text and convey impact and meaning – at a glance.

The main thing to bear in mind here is that images have to be well chosen. If we compare an image to a headline for a

SUNDAY
MONDAY
TUESDAY
WEDNESDAY
THURSDAY
FRIDAY
SATURDAY

moment, they can both grab attention and entice you to 'read on', whether you're using single, full frame shots or creating your own graphics.

Images also send powerful messages, so make sure they support your brand – in both substance and style. Quirky cartoons may be eye catching and fun in certain circumstances, but may not be in alignment with your brand positioning or brand personality.

If you want something professional that goes beyond PowerPoint but stops short of video, then storyboarded static images or stills can be informative and compelling – produced as a Slideshare or video. And an infographic can indeed be used to replace a thousand words – as long as it's well designed.

Audio

As I write this, 'podcasting' is becoming the latest most talked about media option. And audio does indeed have lots of advantages. It immediately gives your audience a richer and more intimate experience. Listening to real voices and real conversations. Hearing your CEO discuss his views on key issues. Hearing one of your customers describe what it's like working with you. In addition, just as images can enhance text, so music can add mood and evoke feeling.

You haven't got the visual element that video gives you, but it is far easier to achieve a professional outcome – not least because you are only working with the dimension of the voice. As soon as you add visual recording, your checklist and performance requirements expand ten-fold. Imagine preparing and rehearsing your CEO for a ten-minute recorded conversation and then what the difference would be if you had to get him comfortable and confident to deliver a professional performance in front of the camera (with apologies to media trained CEOs everywhere).

Video

Video has the power to take the audience experience delivered by audio and deepen it. Done well, this is the closest we can get to experiencing someone or something live, in person. Video can encompass a wide range of different treatments from a short film with cinematic qualities to an animated whiteboard or explainer video – as well as the talking head or in-conversation interview.

It isn't something to adopt lightly – not just because of production quality (which we'll discuss on Thursday), but because you're unlikely to want to make just one great video. If you're serious about content marketing, the formats you choose will be part of your strategic decision making and mean a commitment to an approach and technique over the longer term.

The second dimension – content techniques

With those four basic content formats percolating in your brain, let's drill down a little further into this aspect of 'content experience'.

We can think of the job we want our content to do as being the same as we would want a well-trained, consultative, empathetic sales person to do. Yes, that's right, I did say sales person.

Here, I am visualizing someone who, once they have a clear understanding of their prospect's problem or aspiration, explains options, answers questions and makes sure that, as far as possible, that person is making the right decision for them at that time. That might be to buy there and then. Or it might be to defer their decision, keep looking or buy elsewhere. This sales person behaves in a thoroughly professional manner and because of that and their general helpfulness, they will be remembered and the prospect may well return one day or refer them, even if they never actually become a customer themselves.

This is a one-on-one interaction, guided by the sales person. There may well be more than one contact. Rapport is established, a relationship develops.

Picture that scenario. Then imagine that you are putting 'content' in place of the 'sales person'.

Beyond telling

To be successful at content marketing we have to move beyond 'telling'. We have to do more than just produce content that reads, sounds, and looks like an advertisement.

So let's explore a few content techniques that can give your audience a more engaging experience than just being sold to. By and large you can use each of these techniques to produce content in any (or a least more than one) of the four formats described above. And you can blend and mix these techniques up. When deciding how to present your content, it's time to get out of that 'we always do it this way' rut and have some fun with it.

Take a look outside your industry and see what's going on. What media, information and marketing do you find yourself responding to – how could you adapt that for your own use?

Conversation

In our everyday lives we are surrounded by conversations. It's a very natural way for us to communicate. Presenting conversations is therefore a friendly, non-intrusive technique that our audience can easily tune into.

Examples include structured one-on-one interviews, informal 'on the sofa' conversations, panel debates, Q & As, and hosted 'chat show' style discussions.

These can be used to get across a wide range of messaging and facts, and cover areas of opinion and commentary.

Even if you still have to produce an official statement about something, your conversational content can help spread the word by going deeper and exploring key points or issues.

And it's a good way to enhance engagement with technical content, research findings, and white papers.

Explanation

One really easy way to get out of telling mode is to switch to explaining mode. If you mentally precede your piece of content creation with the words 'Let me explain this to you ...' you immediately change your mindset and what follows will naturally be more engaging.

'How-to' content has long been a mainstay of marketing collateral, but see what happens when you apply this process of explanation to content relating to ideas and thought leadership. It helps your spokesperson or brand come across as authoritative while minimizing the risk of sounding arrogant or preachy.

Demonstration

This takes 'explanation' to a different level and brings in a visual dimension. Essentially you are showing someone how to do something.

No longer is this the preserve of live events and product demos – we can be helpful in so many more ways. Consider a DIY flooring supplier who actually shows you how to measure your floor space, including all those tricky corners and alcoves, and calculate the number of flooring packs you'll need. As a customer, you don't have to just figure it out from the written guide, you can watch Jake the DIY man actually doing it – in a room pretty much like yours.

Education

This DIY flooring example is also a form of education because as well as being able to buy the right number of packs with confidence, the customer has also learnt a new skill – how to measure up the floor space accurately. Education can be a little piece of learning like this or it can be a much bigger initiative.

Identifying and matching a specific thirst for learning with something that we can teach is a powerful content technique – always remembering that part of our definition of content marketing is that it prepares the ground for a sale.

Précis and collation

Just as a proportion of our audience may at times want deep and detailed content, others may be seeking just the opposite. This provides us with a huge opportunity to be helpful, by summarizing and writing or producing 'short' versions of things that can be consumed quickly and easily. This book is one example. You don't want to read the latest content marketing 'bible', you want to grasp the basics quickly.

'Short' can also mean very short. For instance a series of 500-word blog posts or two-minute audios that highlight the key learning points from 'must read' but heavyweight business books.

Rounding up and collating also speaks to the time poor – the top five developments to know about in your niche this year, ten of the most useful tools and resources, the three most innovative ideas published on a specific topic this week.

Content segments

Segments are traditionally used on TV and radio – packaged portions of content, easily identified by the audience and often much anticipated. It could be a 20-second news update in between longer features. Or a regular five-minute slot within a programme that tackles a topic in a specific way. There is usually an element of branding and visual identity associated with segments.

This technique helps to make both you and your content appealing and memorable. You can apply it to sections within a newsletter, recurring features within a campaign, or as a regular slot within your podcast.

If you're used to producing collateral such as a customer magazine, you may already be used to applying segment thinking. 'A day in the life' series is a good way of explaining what goes on behind the scenes, featuring a different job role each time to show the care and attention that goes into creating your product or service from different perspectives.

'Two minutes with ...' or 'Lunch with ...' can badge an interview series within your blog, 'The Friday Rant' a segment within your podcast, or 'Five seasonal tips' a regular feature within your newsletter.

Origination vs curation

Finally, a reminder that you don't have to originate all your own content. You can source, select and share other people's quality content that aligns with your own content strategy and meets the needs and expectations of your audience. The key aspect of content curation though is that you must add value.

So, don't just provide a list in your round up of the ten best pest control blogs so far this year – say why you like them and what the key takeaway points are in each case.

Thinking of sharing a financial market commentary from the BBC or a *New York Times* science report? Explain why you are doing it. Do you have a different perspective or interpretation to offer – or alternative food for thought?

Add your own commentary and points of view. This is *your* content – so we want to hear from you, we want your perspective. Curation enables you to share legally, so make sure you stay legal and quote correctly and avoid plagiarism and copyright infringement.

Bringing it all together

There are many different ways to deliver your content objective. As you progress through the week, keep in mind the diversity of content formats and techniques available to you.

Avoid getting stuck in a rut or default thinking. For example, that a 'newsletter' has to be in a certain format or that, in order to create great 'content', you have to be producing lots of written material.

But equally avoid getting carried away by a whizzy, all bells and whistles approach – just because you can or because someone says you should.

When choosing how to deliver your content, keep 'audience' and 'purpose' firmly in the forefront of your mind. What combination of formats and techniques:

- are best suited to your audience?
- will best enable or trigger your desired call-to-action?
- will best deliver on your content objective – are you setting out to entertain, inform or educate?

Then secondly, think about your content itself and if it naturally lends itself to a particular format or technique.

Summary

Today we've delved a little deeper into the world of content. We've learnt that content can be found everywhere within an organization and that our aim with content marketing is to develop a seamless content experience for our audience – wherever they find us.

We looked at:

- How to decide what content format to use
- The four basic building blocks – text, image, audio and video
- A variety of content techniques we can use to move us beyond telling and selling

We need to keep our content fresh but avoid becoming distracted or misled by the latest, most-talked-about approach. We need to assess if it actually has the potential to work for us.

When it comes to any specific piece of content, choose a format and technique that is well suited to helping you achieve your content objective – what you want your audience to experience, feel or do as a result of engaging with it.

SUNDAY
MONDAY
TUESDAY
WEDNESDAY
THURSDAY
FRIDAY
SATURDAY

It's also easy to overlook the obvious fact that different people like to consume content in different ways at different times, so where appropriate, it's good to offer your audience a choice.

If you now think about the content you already work with, how might you change or develop it to make it more appealing to your audience?

Tomorrow we move on and look at how to develop your content marketing strategy.

Fact-check

1. How do you decide on the best content format to use?
   a) Just produce whatever the CEO says he wants to see ❏
   b) Adopt whatever is currently being talked about on the internet ❏
   c) Consider what is going to give your audience the best content experience ❏
   d) See what your main competitor is doing and copy them ❏

2. Why is it a good idea to give your audience a choice of formats?
   a) Because we all like to consume content in different ways at different times ❏
   b) It's not, because you just don't have time to do that ❏
   c) Because you can – technology makes it easy ❏
   d) It's not, people can just use whatever you decide to give them ❏

3. Do people still like to read in-depth text based content?
   a) No, people just want to look at pictures and listen to sound bites ❏
   b) No, there's no use publishing anything longer than 200 words ❏
   c) Yes, when they've found something they want and find useful ❏
   d) Only if they have nothing better to do ❏

4. What are images really good for?
   a) Distracting people from your copy ❏
   b) Conveying impact and meaning at a glance ❏
   c) Competing with your headline ❏
   d) Making fun of your brand ❏

5. What should be your overall aim when presenting content?
   a) To make it look and sound like an advert ❏
   b) To make it difficult for people to find the answers to their questions ❏
   c) To focus only on what you want to tell people ❏
   d) To mirror what a well-trained sales person with a consultative, empathetic approach would do ❏

6. The technique of explanation is good because
   a) It quickly and easily gets you out of 'telling' mode ❏
   b) It allows you ramble on until you've got nothing left to say ❏
   c) You don't have to think very much ❏
   d) You can easily make stuff up to fill the page ❏

SUNDAY
MONDAY
TUESDAY
WEDNESDAY
THURSDAY
FRIDAY
SATURDAY

7. Why is education a powerful content technique?
a) It allows you to create an e-course – even if no one ever subscribes to it ❏
b) It's not, no one is interested in essentially having to go back to school ❏
c) It gives your content matter experts something to do ❏
d) It allows you to tap into people's thirst for learning ❏

8. How can you be helpful to those with little time to spare?
a) Leave them alone, they've got enough to do ❏
b) Provide a forceful argument on why they should read your latest white paper ❏
c) Provide round-ups and summaries of key topics of interest to them ❏
d) Send them emails every day in the hope that they'll read at least one of them ❏

9. What is a content segment?
a) Easily identified, packaged portions of content traditionally used on TV and radio ❏
b) Something only found in soap operas ❏
c) The bit down the edge of a web page that contains adverts ❏
d) A new form of product packaging ❏

10. Do you have to produce all original content?
a) No, you can just copy and paste stuff from the internet ❏
b) Yes, it's the only way to be credible ❏
c) No, you can curate content and add value by adding your own comments and perspective ❏
d) Yes, otherwise you could be accused of copyright infringement ❏

SUNDAY

MONDAY

TUESDAY

WEDNESDAY

THURSDAY

FRIDAY

SATURDAY

TUESDAY

Develop your content marketing strategy

Today we look at what you need to do and have in place at the strategic level in order to plan, manage and make things happen successfully at the implementation level.

We look at what it takes to fully home in on and understand your audience, find out what makes them tick, how they make their decision to buy from you – and how that helps you with your various content decisions.

We also go a little deeper into buyer behaviour to further develop your thinking before turning our attention to your content marketing goals and how you decide where to deploy your content within your marketing process.

We finish the day with a summary of what to include when you document your content marketing strategy.

SUNDAY

MONDAY

TUESDAY

WEDNESDAY

THURSDAY

FRIDAY

SATURDAY

Putting the customer first

In many ways your content has to do the same job as your product or service – it has to deliver value to the person using it.

It is very easy to approach content the wrong way round. To reach first for the content you already have or concentrate only on what you want to say – without fully considering what your audience really wants to hear about.

We all have a tendency to focus on ourselves – *our* company, *our* people, *our* products, *our* services, what *we* are doing. And as marketers we often get pushed in that direction by various parts of our organization, from the Board to the sales department.

Yes, marketing has to support and drive the achievement of business objectives and sales goals. But we must ensure our messaging and content actually speaks to our audience.

TIP *If we don't consider our audience, we'll be talking, but no one will be listening.*

So, to develop a content marketing dimension to your overall marketing strategy and shape a top line, strategic plan, you need to think carefully about your audience groups and decide how to use content to influence each groups' buyer behaviour.

The work we do today will give overall direction to your content marketing and a framework within which to manage and implement it.

Home in on your audience

As marketers we know our prospects and customers come first. Without them we'd have no business. We have to understand their needs, their problems, their pain points and their aspirations in order to provide products and services that they will want to buy.

You probably already have some sort of target market or market segment analysis in place. But it's more than likely you'll now have to carry out more detailed and in-depth work in order to create useful, distinct 'personas' in order for your content marketing to be successful.

A persona is a detailed portrait or description of a specific group of prospects or customers – a distinct audience that you can reach and influence through content marketing.

Each persona is defined by:

- their unique set of characteristics and interests
- how they decide whether or not to buy or use your product or service
- the stages they go through when making their decision
- and what influences them at each stage.

In order to create truly useful personas we need to go beyond demographics to understand what makes each persona tick. And in a business-to-business market we need to go beyond job titles, to see and get to know the people and the reality of their everyday environment, challenges and priorities.

How do you get this level of detail and understanding?

1 Focus on real people actually within your target market.
2 Avoid falling into the trap of assuming you know what people want or believing that they want what you want.
3 Go and actually meet and spend time with real customers and potential customers.

4 Interview people within your customer facing teams – others who engage directly with buyers and users in a sales, customer service or delivery situation.
5 Use your opt-in subscriber lists to ask questions and carry out appropriate and well thought out surveys.
6 Use social media as a research and 'listening' tool.

How do you create or describe a persona?

What you are aiming for is to describe each persona in enough detail for you to be able to make useful content decisions about them.

It's not an exercise you just do once and then consign your notes to a filing cabinet. Rather you will use it as a planning tool, regularly checking and updating your personas through ongoing contact with your market and customer facing teams and keeping them aligned as your organization's overall business and marketing plan evolves.

How many personas you have depends on the number of market segments you have and the complexity of the decision making process within each.

● Your personas should be separate and distinct from one another – each with a set of common characteristics and behaviours.
● Each persona will have a different decision-making process, governed by different considerations.

- Ultimately, your content strategy will be different for each one – because each one will require different content in terms of what, why, how, when, and where.

If you find you get confused or have problems, questions or gaps when it comes to deciding on and planning your content, revisit your personas because it's likely you've drawn them too superficially and lack understanding in some key areas.

If you end up with a lot of personas, first check that they are indeed separate and discrete groups. If they are, you may then want to assess and select those best suited to a content marketing strategy vs another marketing strategy. Or implement a staged content marketing roll-out in order to effectively manage your resources – an approach which has the added advantage of allowing you to 'learn by doing' over the longer term.

Factors to consider when developing a B2C persona

- Shopping behaviour and preferences
- Media behaviour and preferences
- Social profile – how they relate to family, friends and work colleagues
- Who and what influences them
- How sophisticated they are when it comes to technology
- Meaningful demographic and socio-economic information
- Buying patterns and behaviours
- The different reasons they might buy from you
- Why they would use your product or service in preference to a competitor
- What might stop them buying from you
- Values and beliefs – what's important to them generally
- What motivates them
- What's important to them in relation to your product or service
- What problems they have that you can help them solve
- What aspirations they have that you can help them achieve
- What unique value you can offer them.

Questions to consider when developing a B2B persona

- In their job role, what are they responsible for?
- What are they tasked with achieving?
- What are their challenges, frustrations or problems?
- How do they go about tackling these challenges or resolving these problems?
- What's the environment like that they are working in?
- What are their preferred methods of research?
- What type of media and information do they read or engage with?
- Are they the final decision maker or do they only influence the decision-making process?
- Do they make the decision alone or with others?
- How do they interact with others in the decision-making process?
- Outside of others in the decision-making chain, what are their other sources of information or recommendation?
- If they are an influencer, who do they influence, what type of influence do they have and how strong is it?
- In relation to the type of products and services that you offer, what questions do they ask?
- What language, words and phrases do they use when talking about them?
- Are there any seasonal or other patterns to their purchase behaviour?
- What unique value can you offer this persona?
- Why would this persona want to do business with you as opposed to all the other options open to them?

How does a persona help you when it comes to content?

When defining your content strategy and at the tactical level, there are lots of content decisions to make. Well-crafted personas help with:

- what content topics are likely to be of interest
- the type of stories likely to be most appealing

- the depth of content likely to be of interest
- how best to present this content – formats and techniques
- the best ways to get the content in front of your target persona – either directly or via others
- trigger words or phrases likely to get attention
- keeping your messaging consistent, focused and on track over time
- developing content themes and storylines over time to help refresh and recycle content.

The bottom line is that defining and using personas makes you approach content from the perspective of your customer or prospect and actually gives you the best chance of providing content that they want and that will be of value to them.

TIP *Without personas it's all too easy to slip into thinking about content predominately from your own perspective and get stuck on the 'it's all about us' treadmill.*

Delve deeper into buyer behaviour

I've mentioned the need to understand each persona's buyer or user decision-making process. Using a simple yet powerful communications model like AIDCA helps to add depth and richness to your content strategy.

Awareness (or Attention)
Interest
Desire
Conviction
Action

The original AIDA model was developed by Edward Strong and included in his 1925 book *The Psychology of Selling and Advertising*.

When we are in the process of buying something, we first become aware of it, then we develop an interest in it, then we get a desire for it. It is likely that we are moving away from the purely logical to the more emotional. Then sometimes reality kicks back in at the 'conviction' stage. Is this really the best option, is it the right time, can we afford it?

Ticking the 'conviction' box triggers our intention and converts it into 'action' – i.e. we buy.

If we accept that our customers will be experiencing this sequence (or something similar) when making up their minds about buying from us, there are two key factors at work that will influence their behaviour at each stage – the two Cs of 'confidence' and 'comfort'.

You need to be giving your prospect both the confidence (head or logic centred) and the comfort (heart or emotion centred) they need at each stage in order for them to take the next step and keep on moving forward through the engagement process.

To develop your content marketing strategy, take each of your personas in turn and walk with them through the AIDCA model.

● What does each one need to know, experience and feel at each stage?
● What type of content is most likely to help you achieve this? Think about your core 'what' (information, message or story) and also how best to present it (format and technique).

If you are already using this or a similar model to help develop your overall marketing strategy, you can now add in this content dimension.

One key thing to highlight here is that content marketing is often the ideal means of moving people through the AIDCA stages – especially the latter ones.

Often marketers think their marketing process isn't working because they're not getting enough results at the 'action' end. In reality they could be doing a great job of, for example, raising 'awareness' and converting that to 'interest' only to have people stuck at the 'desire' or 'conviction' stage.

If they get stuck it's because there's something missing – information, a piece of the story, understanding, emotional or practical engagement. Whatever it is, their 'desire' or 'conviction' box has not been ticked – either consciously or subconsciously. And it's holding them up.

This is quite different to having people drop out of your process because they've actively rejected you. Often all you have to do to get them moving again is to supply the missing piece of the puzzle – and using some form of content can be one of the best ways to do this.

Decide what you what to achieve

So far today we've been focusing on your prospects and customers – your audience, the people who will be receiving and consuming your content, even actively seeking it out.

The other side of the equation is to clearly understand and articulate what you want to achieve with your content marketing.

Set content marketing goals

You need to set some content marketing goals and be sure that they are specific and realistic. Typical content marketing goals can relate to:

- building brand awareness and supporting your brand positioning
- generating sales leads
- converting leads (via a call-to-action)
- starting and/or growing an opt-in subscriber list
- nurturing leads
- converting subscribers to customers – whether as an online process or in support of your direct, in-person sales process
- delivering after sales customer service
- retaining customers and fostering customer loyalty over the long term
- up-selling and cross-selling
- supporting referral and recommendation strategies.

Look familiar? Yes, you can obviously use other marketing strategies to achieve these same goals and you are likely to already have a selection of them somewhere in your overall marketing plan.

So, ask yourself:

- What is the unique or incremental value that content marketing (vs other types of marketing) can contribute to each goal?
- What is the specific opportunity in relation to each goal that content marketing (vs other types of marketing) has the potential to deliver?
- Can we achieve more in relation to each goal by enhancing or replacing current strategies with content marketing?

Map your customer journeys

Unless you are a new start-up, you're going to be introducing content marketing into your existing marketing process. Even if to date you haven't consciously designed this process, you will have one. Every company does. Because you have sales people out there working a sales process and you have customers out there buying from you. And those customers will be finding you and finding out about you somehow.

The final piece in today's strategy puzzle is their journey. The path they take to your door. The touch points – the points of contact or interaction with your brand – that they encounter along the way.

In most organizations, the customer journey has two distinct phases – before and after the sales process kicks in.

Before, the prospective customer is interacting with your wider marketing and today is more in charge of how they find, choose and buy products and services than ever before.

As marketers we've always had to decide where and when to place our marketing collateral, activities and events.

So now you need to take each persona and map their customer journey and touch points to:

- help you decide where and when to publish, distribute and promote your content
- tailor your content for the specific platforms and channels you choose to use
- ensure that you achieve a cohesive, joined up process to offset the risk of prospects falling into gaps or becoming stuck in dead ends.

Once their journey takes them into your sales process, then you need to assess how to present and produce your content to enhance this process and support your sales people.

Your seven-point strategy framework

I've taken you through this chapter in a particular way in order to develop your thinking. Just as with any marketing strategy or plan, there's no definitive way to document it.

If you're starting from scratch, document it in a way that makes most sense and is most useful to you. If you already have a robust marketing planning process and plan format in place, then ensure you are updating it appropriately to reflect your new-found content marketing thinking.

Here's a summary of what to include:

1 The case for content marketing. Why you have chosen to adopt this approach and the unique value it will bring to your brand. How it will integrate with your other marketing strategies and activities.
2 A set of specific content marketing goals with an explanation of how you will measure progress towards and achievement of them.
3 An overview of each persona, backed up with the detailed description and an explanation of each persona's typical buyer behaviour pattern and decision making process.
4 A top-line summary of the type of content you propose to deploy to move each persona through the AIDCA engagement process.
5 An indication of the platforms and channels you will use to reach each persona and why you have selected them.
6 How you intend to measure the performance of your content, platforms and channels.
7 Your content marketing budget.

Remember, this is your strategic snapshot – a top-level summary. If you're running a traditional marketing planning process, this is what you will be addressing each year as part of your three-year (or longer) term view.

As we progress through the rest of the week we will cover various content topics in more detail. This will probably mean that you will continue to develop your understanding and clarify your strategic thinking around content, platforms, channels and evaluation.

So, at the end of the week, come back to this strategy framework, review it and add in any points that you feel would be useful and valuable to hold at this strategic planning level.

The 2015 annual 'Content Marketing: Benchmarks, Budgets and Trends' research by the Content Marketing Institute showed that the two main differentiators between the not-so-good and the great content marketers were that they were a) writing their strategy down and b) following it closely on a consistent basis (www.contentmarketinginstitute.com/research).

Summary

Today we've covered the thinking and work you need to do in order to develop a sound content marketing strategy.

We looked at:

● How to fully focus on your audience so that you can make useful decisions about what content to create
  ● The concept of personas and how you actually develop them
  ● How to use the AIDCA model to further understand buyer behaviour
  ● Setting specific content marketing goals
  ● Mapping your customer journeys to help you decide where and when to deploy your content.
    ● What to document – your seven-point strategy framework.

Your content marketing strategy gives you direction, keeps you on course and helps with tactical decisions as new content ideas and options pop up.

If you are introducing a content marketing strategy or extending your current level of content activity, then you will need to integrate your 'content' thinking into your

SUNDAY

MONDAY

TUESDAY

WEDNESDAY

THURSDAY

FRIDAY

SATURDAY

existing marketing plan. This may mean you have to dig deeper into your customers' behaviour, preferences and desires than you have done to date – and get closer to them in order to do so.

Tomorrow we look at content planning – how to manage the creation, production, publication, distribution and promotion of your content.

Fact-check

1. Developing a content marketing strategy gives you
   a) An excuse to spend lots of time out of the office ❑
   b) Something to talk about in marketing meetings ❑
   c) A framework within which to manage and implement your content marketing ❑
   d) A lot of hard work ❑

2. How important is it to fully understand your prospects and customers?
   a) It doesn't matter that much because it wouldn't make any difference to what you already do ❑
   b) It's vitally important to help you create an effective content marketing strategy ❑
   c) Not that important because you've not bothered much about it so far ❑
   d) It might help you, but only if there's a risk you'll miss your sales targets this year ❑

3. What is a persona?
   a) A list of your customers' job titles ❑
   b) A detailed portrait or description of a well-defined, specific group of prospects or customers ❑
   c) Something to do with opera ❑
   d) The demographic breakdown of your market segments ❑

4. How many personas should you have?
   a) One is enough ❑
   b) The more the better – it makes you look busy ❑
   c) It depends on how many distinct audience groups and decision-making processes you identify ❑
   d) It depends on how many customers you have ❑

5. How do personas help you with content marketing?
   a) They help you decide what content topics, formats and techniques will be most appealing ❑
   b) They don't help at all, you can just guess what content to produce ❑
   c) They only help if you get stuck for something to say ❑
   d) They only help if you have to manage some sort of PR crisis ❑

6. What is AIDCA?
   a) An out-of-date advertising model that's of no use today ❑
   b) A communications model that helps you understand your audience's buying psychology ❑
   c) Something that looks impressive in presentations ❑
   d) A form of social media marketing ❑

7. Why is AIDCA useful in developing your content marketing strategy?

a) It helps you focus on what people need to know, experience and feel at each stage of the buying process ❑

b) It's not much use at all because all you have to do is focus on creating awareness ❑

c) It makes you sound knowledgeable when talking with your boss ❑

d) It's a good way to put pressure on your web developers and ad agency ❑

8. What marketing goals can content marketing help you achieve?

a) It can only impact awareness of your brand and your products and services ❑

b) It doesn't really help you achieve any of your goals ❑

c) It's only good for helping you cross-sell once someone has already bought from you ❑

d) All of them, but you have to be clear about the unique value that content marketing can contribute in each case ❑

9. Why is mapping your customer journeys important?

a) It allows you to spend lots of time with the sales team ❑

b) It's not, it's a step you can easily skip ❑

c) It helps you decide where and when to publish, distribute and promote your content ❑

d) It allows you to use your new process mapping software ❑

10. How should you document your content marketing strategy?

a) Write it up as quickly as possible so you can file it away and get on with other stuff ❑

b) Create a strategic snapshot covering all the key areas in enough detail to be useful and valuable ❑

c) Create the biggest document possible to impress the management team ❑

d) Don't bother documenting it, it's easy to remember ❑

SUNDAY
MONDAY
TUESDAY
WEDNESDAY
THURSDAY
FRIDAY
SATURDAY

WEDNESDAY

Get started with content planning

By now you have a good grasp of how to think about and design your content marketing at the strategic level. We also spent some time on Monday thinking about content itself and the various formats and techniques to use when presenting it.

Today, we start to work with the detail – coming up with a number of specific pieces of content for each of your personas and then planning when, where and how to deploy them.

We look at three specific planning tools to ensure:

- each content item you create and publish is aligned with your strategy – your master planning matrix
- you are able to publish to professional standards on a consistent and regular basis – your workflow
- you successfully manage and track your content through all the stages of the publishing process – your editorial calendar.

Your master planning matrix

Your master planning matrix acts as your master control and helps ensure that each item of content you plan to produce has a clear and specific purpose, linked to a specific persona and a specific marketing goal. In other words, it aligns with your content marketing strategy. For each persona map out each item of content to publish, noting:

1 The 'what' – the core topic, message or story this item will deliver (aligned with what each persona needs to know, experience and feel)
2 What content format you are going to use – what version of text, image, audio, video or combination
3 What content technique you are going to use – how best to get your 'what' across
4 Where you will publish it – your primary platform or channel and any other ones
5 What the purpose of this piece is in terms of call-to-action – what you want your persona to do as a result of engaging with it
6 When you will publish it
7 What specific keyword phrases you are going to optimize this piece for (if any)
8 How and where you will distribute it and promote it
9 How you will evaluate it
10 What content marketing goal this piece is designed to impact.

What you are aiming to do is sketch out your content plan in overview with enough detail to make it meaningful. As well as ending up with a list of core content items, you will be able to start to identify things like your most common formats and channels, and how complex your evaluation plan might be. We'll be adding another layer of detail later. For example, here you would plot roughly when you might publish it, say which quarter, month, or season. Later you will assign a specific date.

In terms of time frame, start with the next 12 months and, on a rolling basis, tackle the next 3 or 6 months in more detail than the rest of the year.

A simple example

Let's take a look at a very simple example for a company making eco-cleaning products.

Persona summarized as 'green' consumers motivated to reduce their use of 'toxic', chemical laden cleaning products in the home while maintaining a high standard of hygiene and cleanliness.

Core 'what' – show that our products contain a very small number of non-toxic ingredients and explain the science behind how those ingredients work together as well as the major mainstream brands.

Format – text explanation, image of an 'our' and 'their' pack comparing ingredient listing, audio explanation of science part

Technique – audio interview with one of our product developers

Primary platform/channel – consumer blog on company website

Purpose/CTA – encourage trial/request a product sample

When publish – Spring/April

Optimization/keyword phrase – 'effective eco-cleaning'

Distribution/promotion – Facebook, Twitter, e-newsletter

Other platforms/channels – eco-bloggers, PR

Evaluation – website: referral sources, time spent on page, audio listens, other website pages visited, number of sample requests

Goal impacted – lead conversion, subscriber list growth

A tactical planning process

OK, you may have spotted that this is starting to look a lot like a planning process. The good news is you'll be able to integrate this content element into an existing process fairly easily. However, some companies prefer to keep their content planning separate and even call it something like 'editorial planning', especially if they have got more into the publishing mindset. Whatever you do, you're going to find it more challenging if you haven't already got a robust marketing planning process in place covering your other marketing tactics.

If that sounds like you and you've decided you're going to give this content marketing thing a go, you're going to have to get smarter and at least get a planning process in place for your content. Otherwise you're likely to end up with a hit-and-miss publishing schedule and patchy results.

Be realistic

I've given just one example above and you can see that it won't take many content items before you're planning and managing a fairly complex matrix. How complex depends on the size and complexity of your market, products and services.

The key is to avoid trying to do too much too soon. It's better to build your content marketing muscle slowly and focus on doing a small number of things well – rather than being over ambitious. Otherwise you risk:

- making fundamental mistakes in execution
- producing poor quality content – and there's enough of that out there already
- failing to hit your publishing schedule
- failing to engage your audience
- losing the support of people within your organization.

So taking a pragmatic approach, you could, for example, get started by taking one persona and crafting a very specific 12-month awareness or education programme using one primary platform or channel.

In this way you can also essentially pilot content marketing and use the results to assess how well the approach might work for your company and then plan future strategy and develop your people and skills – based on a more evidence-based business case.

Even if you are keeping it simple, you still need to be realistic about exactly what it takes – time and resources – to create and produce good quality content (as you will see as we work through the rest of today).

Once you've mapped out your master planning matrix, it's time to think about just how your content is going to get produced and published. What are the key steps and tasks involved and what people with what skills do you need to make them happen? This process is known as your workflow.

Designing your workflow

A typical content plan contains multiple types of content, activities, platforms and channels. A workflow is the ordered sequence of steps or tasks required to create, produce, publish, distribute and evaluate your content.

> **TIP** *Having a clear, documented workflow enables you to produce content to time, regularly and to a consistently high standard.*

Even when they have set up a specific content platform or channel, many companies fail to publish to schedule. You'd wonder what was going on if your favourite newspaper or magazine didn't appear one day or if it was littered with blank spaces.

Consciously planning your content as we are today and thinking through your workflow will help you understand exactly what has to happen to get your content out there and who you need in your team to make it happen.

How to identify your workflow

A documented workflow includes:

- the step or task itself
- the role responsible for making it happen
- when it needs to be done – a deadline or a timescale or a lead time.

You may be able to design one workflow that is flexible enough to cover all your content, or it may make sense to have separate workflows if you are managing several activities made up of significantly different steps or tasks. For example, text-based vs broadcast production, online vs printed media.

Map out the steps involved from start to finish. A good way to do this is to use sticky notes and a wall, whiteboard, large piece of paper or table top. Make each step or task as specific as possible – one single step or task on each sticky note. Then arrange them in a logical order. Typical steps include:

1 Identifying your source or input materials
2 Identifying a subject matter expert
3 Assigning roles
4 The different elements of content creation – researching, writing, scripting, designing, or recording
5 Content optimization
6 Reviewing for alignment with guidelines
7 Editing
8 Producing – getting the content looking or sounding good and fit for publication
9 Proofing
10 Legal authorization
11 Signing off
12 Publishing – making the content live
13 Specific channel management
14 Specific channel or platform promotion
15 Evaluation and measurement

Your workflow will include a number of different roles, each responsible for a different set of tasks or part of the process. And these roles may be carried out by different people depending on the type of content and channels you are working with. Someone also has to be responsible for managing the process as a whole.

One of the mistakes that many new content marketers make is to underestimate the steps involved and resources required to actually produce quality content to professional standards. They focus almost exclusively on creating it and then skip happily on to publishing and promotion.

Assess timescales

Once you've mapped out your workflow it's easier to assess how much time is required to complete the whole process properly to schedule. If you work backwards from your publication date, you get a sense of when the preceding steps in your workflow have to happen.

In the beginning, this might involve a fair bit of guesswork but the more you run the process, the more you will be able to fine-tune it – refining timings and also spotting any gaps or missed tasks.

Make it repeatable

The whole point of mapping and documenting this workflow is so that you can repeat it consistently each time to the same standard. Many brand content initiatives fail simply because individuals and teams start from scratch each time. This takes up more time and energy, and usually ends up using more resources.

What you still need to do is think like a professional publisher to make sure you are aware of all the necessary steps and tasks. Consider setting up a visit to your regional newspaper or other media company for half a day and get to know their end-to-end publishing process first hand – and also exactly what the various roles actually entail.

Building your content team

Once you've got this far, the next task is to decide exactly who will be performing the various roles within your workflow.

Chances are you have identified some roles and skills not currently found in your marketing team. If you are managing this team or a particular area of work, you'll have to decide how to manage your resources in order to fill the gaps.

- Who in your team or elsewhere in the company has the skills you now need?
- How might you re-engineer the team to take account of new or enhanced roles?
- Does it make sense to combine roles and re-train or upskill certain people?
- Does it make sense to outsource specific roles or skills to a freelancer?
- Is the role already covered by an existing agency relationship – and, if not, could it be?

If you are an individual within the marketing team or someone who works closely with them, the key question is how you can best use or improve your skills and realize your potential within this new content marketing landscape.

Creating your editorial calendar

The editorial calendar adds a final, practical and detailed layer to your planning. Think of your workflow as your template for how to get your content published on time, time after time. Your editorial calendar then addresses a specific timescale, and adds the detail of who will do what, on specific dates – and tracks progress.

If you're working with a small number of activities or channels, you may only need one editorial calendar. If you've got more going on, then it may be more effective to have a number of editorial calendars for specific activities or channels.

The concept is similar to the tracker you might use to plan and manage other marketing activities such as events, exhibitions, speaker programmes, email marketing, and PR.

What you want to aim for is something that is genuinely useful and avoid creating a complicated monster. If you are already using some sort of scheduling tool, by all means see if you can adapt it for this purpose. Otherwise, I advise starting off with a spreadsheet and the most simple design possible so you get used to using it and learn what works for you – you can always enhance it as you go.

If we take a simple example of an editorial calendar for your blog, your calendar might contain:

- the scheduled publication date
- the author/writer
- the subject matter expert or source (if different from the author/writer)
- the editor and/or the person responsible for sign off
- the post topic
- the title of the published post
- the persona/audience for the post
- the current status (the stage it's reached within your workflow)
- any key dates – for example, the date the draft must be ready for editing or approval.

You may also want to add some of the other items from your planning matrix above. For example, if you want your editorial calendar to act as a useful aide-memoire for your writers, you may want to add:

- the specific call-to-action for the post
- any specific keyword phrases you want to include in the post.

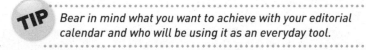
Bear in mind what you want to achieve with your editorial calendar and who will be using it as an everyday tool.

You can use a similar approach to manage and track the distribution and promotion of your content across your various channels and platforms.

Clear thinking required

Take care to remain clear about the purpose of each of these planning tools as you adapt them for your own circumstances.

1 Your master planning matrix helps you create a content plan in overview and ensures that each item of content you create is aligned to a specific audience and has a clear purpose.
2 Your workflow, like a checklist, maps the steps, tasks and roles required to get each type of content published successfully, enabling you to keep to a regular schedule and consistent standards.
3 Your editorial calendar acts as a tracker and gives the practical detail necessary to plan and manage a specific content activity or channel – listing each item of content (e.g. every blog post for the next six months), the person assigned to each role, specific delivery dates and deadlines.

The danger of jumping straight to creating an editorial calendar and ignoring the first two steps is that:

● Without the thought that goes into your master planning matrix, you risk your first focus being an 'internal' one and, continuing the blog example, your posts soon become all about you.
● Without consciously thinking about and designing your workflow, you may miss out important steps and tasks and fail to fully grasp the complete end-to-end process and how long it takes.

Irrespective of how many people are involved, content is a team effort. So, share your plans, workflows and calendars with everyone involved. This has several benefits:

● It helps people understand their role and how they fit in with everyone else – and the consequences of missed deadlines.
● It helps people step in or step up in times of unplanned absences or when circumstances or priorities change.
● It gives visibility to your stakeholders and budget holders, so they know what you are setting out to achieve and how well you are progressing.

If you are recruited into a content team ask to see these plans, workflows and calendars if they are not immediately. Make sure you are not being asked to work in the dark or as part of a disorganized team. ... Unless of course you want to make a bid for getting things set up and properly organized yourself!

Summary

Today we looked at how to get organized and plan at the detailed task level to ensure we create, produce, publish, distribute, promote and evaluate our content successfully.

- Our master planning matrix integrates with our overall marketing planning process and helps us remain focused on our audience and content marketing goals as we plan what pieces of content to publish.
  - Designing our workflow ensures we understand all the steps required to get our content out on time and to a professional standard.
- Creating our editorial calendar allows us to assign specific people and deadlines to specific tasks and manage the whole content process.

The more items of content you publish, the more complex your planning will be. But it is essential if you are going to publish consistently and in line with your content marketing strategy.

This is the point where you are designing and setting up the process that will allow you to execute your strategy successfully.

SUNDAY MONDAY TUESDAY WEDNESDAY THURSDAY FRIDAY SATURDAY

Once up and running, like a well-oiled machine, it will allow you to run, manage, evaluate and refine your content marketing in order to continuously develop it and keep it going over the long term.

Tomorrow we look at content creation in more detail and how to make your content as compelling as possible.

Fact-check

1. What does a master planning matrix help with?
   a) Deciding what date to publish a specific blog post ❑
   b) Ensuring each piece of content has a clear purpose and links to a specific persona and goal ❑
   c) Finding a last-minute filler for your customer magazine ❑
   d) Assessing if you should still be using email marketing in five years' time ❑

2. What would help you when setting up and using a master planning matrix?
   a) Delegating it to your social media team ❑
   b) Having to write an annual report for your board ❑
   c) Already having a robust planning process in place for your other marketing activities ❑
   d) Only thinking about what you have to do next week ❑

3. What is a workflow?
   a) A process made up of tasks, steps, roles and lead times required to publish successfully ❑
   b) A type of electronic time sheet ❑
   c) Something they use in the IT department ❑
   d) A wall planner to record people's annual holidays ❑

4. What typical steps might you find in a publishing workflow?
   a) Taking coffee breaks and lunch breaks ❑
   b) Meetings when you have to explain to your boss why you missed a deadline ❑
   c) Ordering new cartridges for the office printer ❑
   d) Writing, editing and proof reading ❑

5. What does a workflow help you to do?
   a) Take more time off for holidays ❑
   b) Publish consistently to time and to a professional standard ❑
   c) Work out why no one is reading your newsletter ❑
   d) Improve your writing skills ❑

6. How might you effectively resource any new skills required?
   a) Outsource specific roles to a freelancer ❑
   b) Hope for the best and just muddle through ❑
   c) Let an existing team member get on with it without retraining ❑
   d) Not bother – if you don't have the skills, it just won't get done ❑

7. What is an editorial calendar?
a) Something to help you feel like you work in the media ❏
b) Something only used by PR people ❏
c) A detailed publishing schedule for a specific channel like your blog ❏
d) A giveaway from your office supplies company ❏

8. What is always included in an editorial calendar?
a) The dates when you are due to take your agency team to lunch ❏
b) A keyword phrase ❏
c) How much you're paying any freelancers ❏
d) The publication date and the name of the content creator ❏

9. Why is it a good idea to share your plans, workflows and calendars?
a) It's not, you don't want people to know what you're up to ❏
b) It helps everyone involved see how they fit in to the process and the consequences of missing a deadline ❏
c) It keeps you busy ❏
d) It means you don't then actually have to talk to anyone ❏

10. If you're brought into a content team, should you:
a) Expect to have to do everything at the last minute? ❏
b) Just respond to whatever you're asked to do, however ad hoc it seems? ❏
c) Work out how soon you can go to lunch? ❏
d) Ask to see the workflow and editorial calendar? ❏

SUNDAY

MONDAY

TUESDAY

WEDNESDAY

THURSDAY

FRIDAY

SATURDAY

THURSDAY

Create compelling content

As we saw yesterday, taking a piece of content from an idea to publication is a team effort.

It's beyond the scope of this book to teach you specific writing or graphic design skills – there are other books for that. What I want to share today are some of the key principles that underpin the creation of compelling content and how you can put those into practice.

By compelling I mean content that attracts the attention and holds the interest of your audience – content that keeps your audience coming back for more.

What can you do to ensure the content you are creating and producing has appeal, presents your brand in the best light and has the best chance of being shared?

SUNDAY

TUESDAY

WEDNESDAY

THURSDAY

FRIDAY

SATURDAY

Leverage the power of the story

Much is written about the art of storytelling and how effective it is as a technique or framework for creating compelling content.

The human psyche loves a story. Who can forget the sense of anticipation when, as a child, we heard the words 'Once upon a time in a land far, far away ...'?

TIP *Stories have the power to captivate and engage us. Perhaps it's because our subconscious is still on the lookout for the handsome prince or the pot of gold?*

All good stories have a structure – a framework within which you organize your characters, events and detail and tell your story. Whether it's your brand story or a very specific story that addresses one of your persona's problems or aspirations, your story must be believable and have the power to draw in your audience.

A well-known structure is that of the Hero's Journey where the story takes the reader through the stages of:

- Orientation – *This is a story about a King who has a beautiful daughter ...*
- Crisis – *One day the kingdom is threatened by a savage dragon who captures the princess*
- The call – *Our hero, a Prince from another land, arrives to save the day*
- Problems – *Our hero struggles to defeat the dragon, beset by a hoard of the dragon's supporters*
- Resolution – *Our hero defeats the dragon and saves the princess*
- Moral or Conclusion – *Good triumphs over evil and they all live happily ever after*

An online search will give you various versions of the Hero's Journey and you can also use the persuasive AIDCA sequence we met on Tuesday. The key thing is that you understand the structure you are using and how it can impact the power of whatever story you are telling. You can adapt the Hero's Journey for your particular company or content type and express it in language more readily understood by your contributors or writers – for example, to create a case study or article template, or to storyboard a video.

Go where the stories are

In any company, the real stories are rarely found in your office. They are out there on the front line – where your customers are, where those you are helping carry on their everyday lives, where your people interact with them. Good PR people are used to getting out and about, but marketing people less so.

You need to get a clear picture of who your primary content sources are and where they are. Within your own organization, those people are often your content matter experts. The product developers and designers, the engineers, the service deliverers, the front line workers.

Then you need to establish a means of tapping into them and even involving them in the creation process. Blanket initiatives, such as insisting everyone writes a blog post once a month, often fail because of lack of buy-in. Understandably so. Most people have enough to do already and they may be unused to writing or presenting for the type of audience you are addressing. So you will need a well thought-out and planned approach to reach out to and engage your internal content sources.

- Consider the individuals involved. Is there anyone who might actually enjoy sharing their knowledge or aspects of their work in a little more depth or with new audiences?
- Are there groups who perhaps already do this as part of their current role? For example, give tours or talks to visitors or business or school groups. Perhaps they go to industry events and produce some sort of content for internal dissemination? Look for where and how they are already sharing – even though it is in a different context.
- Then consider how you can tap into this – through interviewing them or recording them in action.

- You may find people who are already creating content for their own use. Those who are passionate about their subject. They may be writing a personal blog or journal, or taking photographs of or filming their work. You may find they have valuable content to share and are only too willing to be recruited into your content team.

Sales and customer service people know the most common questions that prospects and customers ask and the advice they seek. They'll usually be happy to talk with you, let you work alongside them for a day and take you out on customer visits. The key thing once again is to make it easy for them to help you get to the heart of those stories.

TIP *Whether you are looking for an idea, to develop a storyline, for facts, opinions, or real life experiences, one moment of insight on or from the front line is worth hours of guesswork at your desk.*

Adopt the mindset and skills of a journalist

Journalists are well known for asking lots of questions and are unafraid of asking tricky or difficult ones. They dig away beneath the surface of a story and come up with new angles – the real 'hook' that's going to appeal to their audience. They have a nose for a story and they are endlessly curious.

When planning your story, when interviewing and when reviewing your own or someone else's work, imagine you are coming to the subject for the first time. Be curious about it. Your reader may see the subject in very different light to you. Ask yourself:

- What's the burning question our audience is asking about this subject right now?
- How does it impact their lives?
- How can we best answer that question for them?
- How does our message or opinion relate to them?
- What's the key takeaway for them?
- What's the real story here?

Once they've got the story, a journalist then knows how to write or present it in order to hold the attention of their audience. They work out the main point of the piece and they get to it quickly, then the rest of the story unfolds.

Create and maintain a consistent voice

We've discussed how content marketing is all about building relationships and trust over the long term. Just as we want to hold our audience's attention during the sharing of one story, so we want to hold it for the duration of our time together. That means maintaining the same voice – the same distinctive tone and style – across all our content marketing efforts. We need the same brand personality to turn up time after time. This means you need to be clear about what that personality is in the first place and then ensure your content always reflects it.

To do this you need to have a process and materials in place in order to brief your content creators and implementers effectively – not just to keep a consistent voice but also to ensure they conform to standards and deliver to your expectations.

If you already have brand guidelines, that's good but make sure they are fit for purpose when it comes to, what could now be quite a different set of content items – and crucially more people with more diverse roles creating it. If you haven't issued a specific brief, you can't really complain if your guest contributor provides a 1500 word blog post with language that's too technical for your audience when you were expecting 500 words of chatty repartee.

- Ensure everyone knows what you mean by basic terms such as article, case study, blog post or video script.
- State any specific criteria. Equally make it clear what can be included or done at the author's discretion.
- Provide guidance on word count or length.
- Make it clear what persona or audience the piece is aimed at.
- Explain the desired tone and style – whatever the media format, whether text or image based.
- Give deadlines.
- Say if and how their work may be edited.

Always aim for a professional standard

A bit like ensuring a consistent voice, this means first defining your production standards and then ensuring that you adhere to them. You also need to understand what it takes to achieve those standards. However funny, quirky or eye catching a piece of content, you'll fail to hold your audience's attention if the quality of the piece falls below a certain standard – because it won't be fit for purpose. Not only will it not do its job of communicating effectively, your audience is likely to make a value judgement, consciously or unconsciously, about your brand if your content is slipshod and comes across as unprofessional – whether that's a rambling story, a poorly composed image, or text with typos.

Be clear about production values

There are some types of content that you are more likely to outsource than others. Video production, for example. If you're outsourcing anything to an agency or a specialist, then you are benefiting from their expertise. However, learn enough about the subject in order to make informed decisions and be able to manage the process properly. Taking video as an example, know what standard or production value you need for your publication or distribution platform. Understand how your video may need to be adapted for different devices. You want your audience to have the same quality of user experience, wherever and however they are consuming your content.

Ensure your content is well written

This means ensuring that each piece has a clear purpose, with a clear audience, is well structured, uses language appropriate for your audience in simple, uncomplicated sentence structures. Well written content is easy to read and understand. Very few marketing communications professionals actually have much, if any, writing training or coaching. As well as improving technique, good training can also help you write better faster, and show you how to improve key aspects like planning and structuring your pieces and ensuring clarity and understanding from the reader's perspective.

Ensure your visual content is well designed

There are lots of free and low-cost tools around that allow you to manipulate images and create graphics easily and quickly. But DIY tools can equal DIY results if used by someone with few design or layout skills. Well-composed and well-designed images can make a huge difference to content performance – helping to attract attention and encourage sharing. Just make sure yours are of an appropriate standard. You can always get templates designed by a professional graphic designer for use by a less skilled person to ensure consistency and quality, especially for high volume usage like social media or blog posts.

Pay attention to the gap between origination and publishing

Whatever your content format, whether written material, audio or visual, the job's a long way from done when the first draft appears. Professional publishers put content through a rigorous 'polishing' process so that the end result is as good as it can be whilst still hitting the deadline. This means editing and proofing, checking facts, grammar, keyword phrases, alignment with style guidelines, and ensuring legal compliance.

Rehearse, rehearse, rehearse

There are very few people who can actually perform well 'off the cuff' and it's a mistake to believe that rapid content creation means just turning on a microphone or pointing a camera and playing it by ear. You wouldn't walk on stage in front of a thousand people without preparing your material and rehearsing, so your audio and video performances should be no different if you want to achieve a professional outcome. Whether you are filming a short 'talking head' or 'in conversation' video or recording a podcast, here are some tips for preparing well whilst keeping some flexibility and achieving a natural outcome.

● Create a logical framework for your piece in the same way you'd structure a written article or write bullet points to manage a talk or presentation. This might be a brief outline of the story you are going to tell or a short list of questions you are going to ask and have answered.
● For a 'talking head', work with your spokesperson to ensure they understand the audience for and the purpose of the piece, and create a loose script to help them stay on message and keep on track with the story.
● For an 'in conversation', let the interviewer lead and be the one who manages the direction and flow of the conversation, adapting questions to get the value you want out of it.
● For video, make sure your performers rehearse (with or without you) to get used to the material before performing the piece on camera for the first time. Unless they are used to being filmed, allow time for them to do some practice runs to get used to the camera environment, especially if you are using a studio.
● Take the advice of the camera operator or person acting as director when it comes to where people should sit or

stand and how they should interact with the camera – they know how to make even the nervous come across to best advantage.

- For audio, consider supporting people with voice coaching. Just a short time practising with a voice coach can help correct the wide range of little issues we all experience when talking into a microphone.

Tailor your content to suit your publishing platform

Think for a moment as a consumer of content rather than as a creator. What are the media, platforms and networks you use and visit on a regular basis? They're probably quite diverse and you're used to reading, hearing and seeing things in certain ways depending on where you are.

In the early days of the web, many companies created their first website by simply taking their existing corporate brochure and turning it into static website pages. We wouldn't dream of doing that today and yet we still sometimes fall into the trap of creating something once and then publishing it in several different places without adapting it and without much thought about what it will look like there.

Avoid simply replicating a piece of content or auto-posting it across different platforms, rather craft it specifically for each place. It might need no more than a little tweaking, but the effort will be worth it. It will look like it belongs and will have the best chance of being noticed, picked up and shared.

Furthermore, your audience may be in a very different state of mind in different places – Facebook vs Twitter vs LinkedIn, for example. This may mean you have to present your story slightly differently in different places. For instance a short, well-chosen clip from your video on Facebook or LinkedIn vs the full video on your website or YouTube channel, or a different tone of voice on Twitter vs LinkedIn.

Create content that people will want to share

Sharing is something that we all, generally speaking, like to do. So as well as creating content that your target audience finds useful, valuable and entertaining themselves, think about what they might also want to share.

A study by The New York Times Customer Insight Group revealed five motivations for sharing:

1 To bring valuable and entertaining content to others: 49 per cent say sharing allows them to inform others of products they care about and potentially change opinions or encourage action and 94 per cent carefully consider how the information they share will be useful to the recipient.
2 To define ourselves to others: 68 per cent share to give people a better sense of who they are and what they care about.
3 To grow and nourish our relationships: 78 per cent share information online because it lets them stay connected to people they may not otherwise stay in touch with, while 73 per cent share information because it helps them connect with others who share their interests.
4 Self-fulfillment: 69 per cent share information because it allows them to feel more involved in the world.
5 To get the word out about causes or brands: 84 per cent share because it is a way to support causes or issues they care about.

Source: The New York Times Customer Insight Group, The Psychology of Sharing: Why Do People Share Online? See http://nytmarketing.whsites.net/mediakit/pos

So, when you're coming up with content ideas, crafting your stories, and looking for interesting angles, think about this list and how you can appeal to one of those motivations.

Summary

None of us want to produce bland, dull, ordinary content so today we looked at some of the key principles that underpin the creation and production of compelling content. That's content that attracts the attention and holds the interest of your audience. Content that they find irresistible.

Today we have looked at the following:

- How to leverage the power of storytelling
- How to uncover and tap into the real stories hidden within your organization
- How thinking like a journalist will help you craft your story
- How to maintain a consistent voice to hold your audience's attention
- How to achieve professional content standards
- How to tailor your content to engage people across different platforms
- How to create content that people want to share

We're no longer at the stage where content is scarce and it's exciting just to be able to sign up for a free newsletter or download a PDF. Your content is competing for your

SUNDAY
MONDAY
TUESDAY
WEDNESDAY
THURSDAY
FRIDAY
SATURDAY

audience's attention. You need to achieve a healthy balance of substance and presentation in order to have the impact you desire. And each content item must be of a defined, consistent, and appropriate standard – well-written and well-produced.

Once you've created your content it's time to get it out there. Tomorrow we consider the key aspects of distributing and promoting your content.

Fact-check

1. What is the Hero's Journey?
a) A TV show on Netflix ❏
b) A framework for telling a compelling story ❏
c) A children's storybook ❏
d) The title of the next Bond film ❏

2. What's a good way of getting story detail from one of your subject matter experts?
a) Keep emailing them until they give in ❏
b) Tell them they have to write it up themselves or you'll tell their boss ❏
c) Arrange a convenient time to go and interview them ❏
d) Waylay them at the coffee machine ❏

3. What are all good journalists good at?
a) Being annoying ❏
b) Spending a lot of time travelling the world ❏
c) Giving PR people a hard time ❏
d) Being curious and asking lots of questions to uncover the real story ❏

4. Why is it a good idea to fully brief your content creators?
a) To ensure they know exactly what you want them to deliver ❏
b) It's not, it takes too long and you can't spare the time ❏
c) It's a good excuse for another meeting ❏
d) So they can adopt whatever tone and style suits them ❏

5. Does achieving a professional standard every time matter?
a) No, on the web no one cares about quality ❏
b) Yes, because sloppy content reflects badly on your brand ❏
c) No, it only matters if it's so bad it's unusable ❏
d) No, because no one will remember what they've seen previously ❏

6. What is a feature of 'well written' content?
a) It's designed to make you laugh ❏
b) It uses language a 12-year old would understand ❏
c) It is well structured to make it easy to read and understand ❏
d) It's very short ❏

7. Is it OK to create something and then publish without further checks?
a) Yes, hitting the deadline is the most important thing, irrespective of quality ❏
b) Only if there's no one available to check it ❏
c) Yes, no one will notice if there's a few mistakes or it could be improved ❏
d) No, editing and proofing are important steps in the publishing process ❏

8. How important is it to rehearse before filming a video?
   a) It's vitally important in order to achieve a natural, professional outcome ❏
   b) It's not important at all, it's better if you don't prepare ❏
   c) It's only important if you're talking about a sensitive topic ❏
   d) It's unimportant because it's the camera operator's job to make you look good ❏

9. What's the challenge when publishing on different platforms?
   a) Sourcing enough quirky images ❏
   b) There isn't one, you just replicate the same piece of content everywhere ❏
   c) Adapting your content to look good and be effective on each platform ❏
   d) Finding enough entertaining content to post on social media ❏

10. A key motivation for people to share content online is
   a) They need to do something while waiting for the train or plane ❏
   b) They want to appear busy ❏
   c) They want to get the word out about causes or brands ❏
   d) They want to impress the people they work with ❏

SUNDAY

MONDAY

TUESDAY

WEDNESDAY

THURSDAY

FRIDAY

SATURDAY

FRIDAY

Get ready to share

Having addressed strategy and planning earlier in the week, we now look more closely at the distribution and promotion of your content.

It's a myth that if you simply focus on publishing good quality content, then your audience will beat a path to your door.

You've put a lot of time, effort and resources into creating and producing your content, so don't neglect it now and allow it to languish unnoticed on your website. You need more than just a few tweets to get it out there, picked up, consumed and shared.

Today we consider some of the techniques commonly used to distribute and promote content and the key things you need to think about in each case.

Get your content noticed

A key mistake many companies make is failing to do enough to get their content out there and in front of their audience. Even though you might well be publishing quite a lot of your content, if not all of it, online, you still have to draw people's attention to it.

Otherwise it's like producing a well-designed, well-written, beautifully printed brochure and keeping the supply under your desk waiting for someone to ask for it. Or simply putting a few copies in reception (if you have offices) for visitors to pick up should they happen to stop by for any reason.

Although you can reasonably expect people to find your online content through search or by visiting your website, you also need to get it noticed by having a specific plan for distributing it and promoting it. Depending on the type of content asset you've produced, you can also make it (or a version of it) available as part of your other marketing strategies or activities.

Equally something that you've produced for, say, an exhibition or a conference like a show reel, giveaway, speech or presentation can be turned into useful online content.

Here are some of the key aspects to consider when managing the distribution and promotion part of your content marketing process.

Owned, paid and earned media

One way to think about and plan content distribution and promotion is to use the three-point 'owned, paid and earned' model. If you're using a lot of platforms and channels, it's a useful way of grouping them up.

Owned refers to media that you wholly own and manage – your website, your blog, your social media accounts, your video channel, your newsletter and magazines, and so on. OK, you don't actually own platforms like Twitter and Facebook in the same way that you own your website, but you do have control over your accounts and, within the differing rules of each platform, control over what you publish and share there.

Paid means anything that you pay for in order to get your content noticed – advertising, sponsored or promoted content, and paid search. 'Native' advertising is any paid item that matches the design and style of the media it appears in and therefore appears more like editorial than actual advertising. It tends to blend in with the content that surrounds it and hence it can be more persuasive than an obvious advert.

Earned is essentially any means by which your content gets distributed and promoted because it's earned it, i.e. it's worth sharing. This covers quite a range from traditional PR and being picked up by bloggers and influencers to being shared by individuals on social media.

Earned is often referred to as the area where you need to work the hardest because it means creating good content that people actually want to share and that is easy to share. But frankly you shouldn't be producing any other sort of content anyway. What is true is that 'earned' distribution and promotion is the one that is best for building credibility and trust in your brand and your products and services – in much the same way as true editorial exposure has always held the edge over advertising and advertorial.

Look at the big picture

Even when companies wake up to having to put effort into distributing and promoting their content as well as creating it, it's still easy to think too narrowly about just how to do this. Remember your content marketing strategy is part of your overall marketing strategy. It may over time become your *leading* strategy, but it will still be integrated with and supported by your other marketing activities – offline and online. Therefore when planning how to get your content out there, consider all ways and means of doing so.

For example, a white paper can be turned into both an online download and a printed document for your sales people to use as a leave behind. Extracts can be used for a series of blog posts, promoted through social media channels and also used in trade exhibitions, email marketing and/or direct mail campaigns. If valuable or niche enough it could also be used as a subscriber incentive, with sign-ups converted via optimized landing pages and a degree of paid advertising. And you can seek influencer endorsement for and comment on your white paper and reach out to partners and stakeholders to ask them to share it as well as using traditional PR.

Build your own audience

Essentially your content is pretty useless if it doesn't have an audience. And there's nothing like having a close, loyal audience of your very own – an audience that has already taken some sort of action to show you that they are interested in what you have to offer. In other words your own, opt-in subscriber list – one of your most valuable assets. Unlike social media followers and connections, you know who each of these people really are, you have their details securely held in your own system, and you can communicate with them directly in various ways. No third party can take this audience away from you. Plus they are already 'engaged' to some degree and in many cases already fans.

Therefore it makes sense to focus resources on growing this list, ensuring you remain targeted on your specific personas and prioritize quality over quantity.

 Your own opt-in list is likely to be your most responsive and fertile content marketing channel through which to distribute and promote your content and get shares and feedback.

Use social media effectively

You can use many social media platforms both as a place to publish content and as a means to distribute and promote it. This means it's versatile but also that you can end up in a bit of a muddle if you're not careful. Let's look at LinkedIn as an example.

1 You can publish a post – an article published directly on LinkedIn itself.

2 You can also share an update in order to promote and link to an article on your own website.

3 In addition, other people can share both your post and your update with their connections and in the case of your post, they can also share it on other social media platforms.

So, when you're considering how to use social media, aim for clarity. Simply having a note in your editorial calendar or distribution plan that says 'LinkedIn' is not good enough – you need to be much more explicit. Especially if someone is going to pick up your workflow at the point of publication. Without clear instructions, what exactly might they do with the article in this example if their only clue is 'LinkedIn'?

Once you're clear about how you are using any one social media platform, make sure you know all the tips and tricks to posting on it – from how to write text and tailor visuals to achieve maximum impact, to when and how often to post.

> **TIP** *You can find lots of useful statistics on social media posting, but remember what really matters is what works for you.*

It's important to use any advice as a guideline and experiment to find out what's most effective for you in practice. Ideally assign a specialist to manage and evaluate your key social media channels and stay on top of trends.

Use specific landing pages

A landing page is a specific web page that has just one purpose – to convert. The design, layout and copy work together without distraction to present a clear yes/no decision – subscribe or leave. It plays a crucial role in persuading people to take that final step to get their hands on your content offer – usually for a valuable content asset such as a white paper, book, or course, in electronic format or print, free or paid-for.

A landing page is concise, well crafted and persuasive. You can create different versions for each persona or niche audience or channel by focusing on different benefits, customizing the headline, and using very targeted language, graphics and images.

The promise and content that sent your visitor to your landing page should be matched by the offer and content on the landing page. For example, if your promotional e-shot promises a 'free ten-part e-course to help introverts become confident networkers' ensure your landing page uses the same headline or strapline, features the same image and reinforces your e-shot messaging.

Consider paid advertising

The idea of promoting your content using paid advertising can be very seductive – especially if you have a marketing background in which brand and product advertising features heavily. And it can work well if it's planned and managed well – but don't think it's the easy option.

- Use it in support of your most valuable content goals and select your best and most appropriate content. For example, a goal that is a specific and measurable step towards a sale or some other significant conversion.
- Maximize your ad spend by ensuring that all the elements and steps in your advertising and conversion process are as good as they can be – landing pages, copy, graphic design, ad monitoring and performance.
- Just because technology and online platforms make it easy for you to 'do it yourself', it doesn't mean producing an effective advert is easy. The devil is in the detail, especially online where one word or a specific colour or call-to-action can make the difference between an advert that works and one that fails. Get to know the relevant best practice and ensure you are using people with appropriate skills.

Encourage sharing

So, you've got a compelling piece of content ready to share. When it comes to distributing and promoting it, make sure you are doing all you can actually encourage and persuade people to do just that, share it.

- When you post on social media sites, customize those posts and links using the format of the specific platform to best advantage. For example, if you are promoting your latest blog post, how and what you post on Facebook should be different to how and what you post on Twitter. Avoid auto-posting across platforms. Optimal text length and image dimensions are different. Take special care with visuals and crop or size them to display to full effect on each platform.

- Make those posts compelling in themselves – not only does it give the reader a reason to click to read, they're more likely to be happy to share something enticing than something bland.
- Likewise ensure content like blog posts have appealing meta descriptions – that's the bit that many social sites pull in when displaying linked content.
- On social media, reference specific influencers, contributors, or sources mentioned in your original piece of content to encourage them to share it.
- Make it easy for your website visitors to share – ensure your web page social share buttons are easy to spot.
- Don't rely on default share messages. Customize yours to be effective. If the share is to Twitter, for example, ensure the share message includes your @handle. I'm very happy when I hit a Twitter share button and I'm presented with a well-designed Tweet and a little disgruntled if I have to tailor it myself for it to be effective. I may just not bother.
- Promote more than once. Keep promoting specific content items across your various platforms. Not everyone is going to see it the first time and you can present and introduce it differently as you reuse and recycle it, mixing it up with your newer and more time sensitive posts.
- In your monitoring, keep track of individuals who regularly share your content and reward them with a friendly comment or thank you every now and again – a little interaction goes a long way and will make you stand out from the crowd.

Use pre-scheduling wisely

Opinion is somewhat divided on whether or not it's a good idea to automate or pre-schedule the distribution of your content. As with many aspects of marketing it rather depends on how well it's done. Whatever the scale of your content operation, a degree of sensible automation can help make efficient use of your time.

- Avoid obvious repetition – schedule different versions of the same post when re-posting. Especially when you've just released something new like a blog post and you are promoting it frequently during the first week or so of publication.
- Don't schedule too far in advance – pay conscious attention to setting up your schedule at regular intervals. This helps ensure you don't post out of date content without noticing or inadvertently post something inappropriate in relation to a sensitive breaking news story.
- Don't auto-post across social media channels; as we've seen one size does not fit all. Set up separate schedules using a tool like Buffer that allows you to easily customize posts for different platforms.
- Don't automate everything. Ensure there's a degree of real time content posting going on, especially in response to real time conversations and questions on social media.
- Monitor what's going on constantly – automating part of your process doesn't mean setting it up once and then allowing it to happen on unattended auto pilot. No technology is foolproof and if human error has crept in, you want to be on hand to put it right.

Understand content optimization

All week we've been talking about compelling content that your audience finds useful, valuable or entertaining and that ideally they want to share. If your content is being picked up, read, watched, listened to, engaged with, linked to and shared, then you are already optimizing it for your audience. Today it is 'natural' engagement factors like these that are increasingly influential with search engine algorithms.

Keyword phrases are still important but primarily because these are the phrases that represent the topics, specific information and answers that your audience is seeking – in the language that they are using when searching. People who find your content through search engines are also important because, usually, they arrive with much more intent and willingness to engage – after all they've just found what they have been looking for.

So the main thing is to continue to understand and write for your particular audience – doing your research at the start of your content planning and creation process.

TIP *Make sure you have a stage in your workflow when you sanity check your draft content and publishing protocols for current search best practice – and keep up with emerging trends.*

Promote internally

So far we've been talking about reaching outside of your organization. Remember also to distribute and promote your content internally and with stakeholders and associates so that everyone is aware of it and has the opportunity to share it with their networks in a timely fashion.

- Encourage sharing by making sure people know the rules. Revisit your social media policy or communication guidelines to check that you've got this aspect covered and consider raising awareness of what you would like them to do from time to time in order to encourage them.
- Be even more specific with your sales team and brief them regularly on upcoming content. Plan updates about content in the same way you would communicate an upcoming marketing campaign for a new product launch or event.

Summary

Today we've looked at the key aspects to consider when managing the distribution and promotion of your content – an important part of your content marketing process and one that's often neglected by many companies.

We covered:

- What 'owned, paid, and earned' media means
- How content can be made available by various means throughout your organization
- Why building your own opt-in mailing list is important
- How to use social media effectively to promote your content
- Why you should use landing pages
- Key considerations when using paid advertising
- How to encourage sharing
- How to use pre-scheduling wisely
- The key things to understand about optimization
- How to encourage your colleagues to share your content.

This is another area where joined-up thinking is key. Avoid narrow or short term

SUNDAY
MONDAY
TUESDAY
WEDNESDAY
THURSDAY
FRIDAY
SATURDAY

planning. Distribution and promotion can and should extend across the whole range of your marketing and sales activities. Some content assets have the potential for a long shelf life, working hard online and as part of offline or in person events – as long as they are reviewed and updated regularly.

Tomorrow, we move on to the final piece of our content marketing puzzle and look at the area of measurement and evaluation.

Fact-check

1. What type of channel best builds credibility and trust?
   a) Owned media – it's yours so surely people believe you ❑
   b) Paid media – a lot of the time you don't even know it's an advert ❑
   c) Earned media – because it shows your content is worth sharing ❑
   d) None of them are that good ❑

2. What's one of the best ways of building an audience for your content?
   a) Post every day on Twitter ❑
   b) Build your own opt-in subscriber list ❑
   c) Ask your salespeople to hand out your newsletter ❑
   d) Get your CEO on local radio ❑

3. When it comes to content, social media is
   a) A versatile place to both post and promote your content ❑
   b) A waste of time ❑
   c) The only way to distribute your content ❑
   d) Only good for sharing photos ❑

4. Why would you use a landing page?
   a) To make a long, complicated sales pitch ❑
   b) To display a photo of your customer service team ❑
   c) To return a 'thank you' message ❑
   d) For conversion – to encourage someone to take a specific action ❑

5. When would you use paid advertising to promote your content?
   a) Whenever you need quick sales ❑
   b) To promote your best content and support high value goals ❑
   c) When it's a video of your CEO announcing your annual results ❑
   d) Just before the start of the weekend ❑

6. What can you do to encourage people to share your content?
   a) Nothing – people either will or they won't ❑
   b) Keep on tweeting 'Read our latest blog post' ❑
   c) Customize social media posts for each platform and make them enticing ❑
   d) Auto-post to as many social media platforms as possible ❑

7. Is it a good idea to pre-schedule the distribution of content?
   a) Only as long as you consciously set up your schedules and monitor them frequently ❑
   b) Yes, schedule as far ahead as possible and then leave on auto pilot ❑
   c) Yes, because then you can just repeat the same social media post over and over again ❑
   d) Yes, because then you avoid having to turn up in real time on social media ❑

8. Content optimization means
a) Writing specifically for search engines ❏
b) Needing to go on a course to understand the Google algorithm ❏
c) Producing content that your audience easily finds, engages with, links to and shares ❏
d) Having to write in a very unnatural style ❏

9. Is it worth promoting your content internally?
a) No, no one internally is interested in what you produce ❏
b) Yes, it gives your people the opportunity to share it with their networks in a timely fashion ❏
c) Only when you're desperate ❏
d) Only when your boss tells you to ❏

10. Do you have to promote content that you publish on your website?
a) No, people will just find it when they visit your home page ❏
b) It depends how big your website is ❏
c) Yes, relatively few people will notice it unless you actively promote it across other relevant channels ❏
d) No, you just need to rely on Google to index your web pages ❏

SUNDAY

MONDAY

TUESDAY

WEDNESDAY

THURSDAY

FRIDAY

SATURDAY

SATURDAY

Learn how to measure success

Today we tackle measurement and evaluation. This is traditionally a challenging area for many marketers. We want to know how well our marketing is performing but it's not always easy to measure. Meanwhile, sales, finance and the management team are chasing us to find out what marketing is contributing to the bottom line.

At least with content marketing the measurement part is easier because much online activity is trackable and therefore measurable. In fact there's almost too much choice, so working out what to measure and why is key.

Today we look at the main principles of successful content marketing measurement and evaluation, the methods and tools available to help us, and how to report results for our own use and to satisfy others.

Meaningful measurement

Once you've got your content marketing up and running you're going to want to know if it's working. Just how successful it is as a strategy. And also how well each of the different parts of your process are performing.

If you have brought content marketing into your marketing mix, how you approach this will depend on how you are currently monitoring, measuring, and evaluating your other marketing strategies and activities. What you essentially need to do, as with your planning, is to develop a content layer within your existing evaluation process and reporting.

Whether you are building on an existing evaluation process or starting with a clean sheet, let's first go back to basics.

- The most important thing is to think about measurement and evaluation at the planning stage. Get clear about what you want to measure and why – before you start implementing.
- Choose measurements that show you how well you are progressing towards the achievement of your goals.
- The ultimate question for many will be what is content marketing achieving in terms of sales – in the same way that, at the top level, that's most likely the question being asked about marketing generally.

So, as you develop your content marketing strategy, think about evaluation at every stage. You've looked at your persona customer journeys and your marketing and sales process. Then you made a deliberate decision to bring content marketing into that mix. When developing your master planning matrix, you mapped what content you were going to deploy, with what purpose, at what time and through which channels.

When thinking about measurement and evaluation:

- First think about what you want to happen at each of the touch points in your process – the points where audience meets content. What counts as a measure of success? Then work out if and how you can measure that. And make that measurement meaningful. This means measuring some sort of content consumption, engagement or sharing.

● Then think about where each specific touch point sits within this process. How well is your content performing in terms of moving your prospect through the process? This means measuring response to a call-to-action or a conversion.

What do we mean by meaningful?

Essentially this is making sure that the metric you are looking at is a true indicator of what you want to measure.

Let's take engagement as an example. If by this you mean how well a piece of content, say a blog post, 'engages' your audience – how interested they are in the topic and how well it pulls them in to your website, then 'page views' or numbers of page visitors is not that meaningful. The time spent on the page is a better indicator, along with specific actions taken (such as clicking on internal links to related content, or social shares) and where else people go on leaving the page (behaviour flow).

It's very easy to get bogged down in meaningless metrics, so carefully choose a small number of meaningful ones to track.

> **TIP** *Be guided by measuring effectiveness or impact, not just quantity of transactions or events.*

Eco-cleaning example

Take a moment to return to and re-read the simple example we looked at on Wednesday for the company making eco-cleaning products. Our measurement and evaluation thinking would go something like this:

Overall measures of success:

1 How interested people are in our topic (how appealing/popular is our chosen story angle).

2 How successful the post was in triggering the CTA (request a product sample).

Website:

● How many visitors and what percentage of visitors came to the page via which social media channels – Twitter and Facebook?

- How many visitors and what percentage of visitors came to the page via our e-newsletter?
- How many visitors and what percentage of visitors found the page via search?
- How many visitors and what percentage of visitors came to the page via other sources – other blogs, online media?
- Did visitors read the post – how long did visitors spend on the page?
- Did the audio add value, did visitors listen to it – how many and what percentage clicked to listen?
- How many and what percentage clicked to request a product sample?
- How many completed the product sample fulfilment process and therefore converted to a lead and got added to our opt-in subscriber list?
- Were there any differences by referral channel (Twitter/Facebook/e-newsletter)?
- Have we generated any new awareness/interest – what percentage were first time vs returning visitors?
- What was the behaviour flow of visitors to this page (where did they go next on the site or did they exit)?
- Were there any differences by referral channel (Twitter/Facebook/e-newsletter) or first time vs returning visitors?

Social

- Number of shares and likes/favourites.
- Detail of comments when sharing or comments left on Facebook.
- Pick up and coverage by eco-bloggers.

Email

- E-newsletter opens, clicks and forwards.

PR

- Pick up and placement in consumer, specialist and trade media.

Therefore

- How many new subscribers did we add to our opt-in list?
- How many leads did we generate?
- How many of these leads eventually converted to a sale, at what total value?
- What were the most successful website referral sources?

This example looks at just one piece of content. Remember each content item has a role to play in your process and should directly link to or impact at least one content marketing goal.

Measurement methods and tools

Having now got an understanding of what to measure, let's consider what tools we have at our disposal to help us.

TIP *If you do any sort of web search for content marketing measurement tools, you'll uncover quite a long list. Once again, choose a small number and use them wisely. Most web tools are free or have a free version or free trial period so you can experiment before signing up to paid plans. However, before going off in search of new tools, make sure you are putting the ones you already have to best use and are using them to track meaningful, customized information – rather than just glancing at default reports.*

- **Website analytics:** If you've got a website, then you've got some form of web analytics – most likely Google Analytics. Take the time to find out exactly what it can do for you. Get yourself on a basic training course where you can take along your own strategy and plan and create a useful set of customized metrics. With Google Analytics you can see where people come from and what they do and where they go when on your site. You can also track specific 'goals' and 'events' to measure how often visitors take certain actions – like sign up to something, download something, click on a specific icon. In other words you can measure specific conversions.
- **Email marketing analytics:** If you're using an email marketing system, use the analytics to measure the performance of your newsletters and e-shots as a content channel as well as interest in the content they contain. If you are linking to website content, you can track who clicks to read or view.
- **Social analytics:** As well as looking at the analytics within your specific accounts, consider using one or two other social tools like Buzzsumo that shows how your website content is

shared across social networks, or Buffer to see what posts are getting you the most shares, likes and comments.

- **Your CRM:** If you have a CRM or some other contact management or sales system, then review what you are currently tracking and see how you might add in or link to your content. For example, if your sales people are using or linking to specific content items in their sales process, networking or social selling activities. Track what content prospects and customers have been exposed to in the same way you would specific marketing campaigns or events.

- **More sophisticated, integrated, end-to-end systems:** Once you've got more experience with content marketing, you may want to consider upgrading to more powerful technology. Once again there are a number of systems on the market, typically described as inbound marketing and sales systems or automated sales and marketing systems. They allow you to set up and manage the whole of the marketing and sales funnel, tracking not just aggregated general trends but the behaviour of individual subscribers. Check out Hubspot, Infusionsoft or Marketo (to name but three) to get a sense of what they can do. Naturally such systems require a significant investment, so it's important that you first hone and fully understand your own marketing process. Then choose what technology you need to support it.

- **Sales insights:** Putting analytics and tools to one side, let's not forget the low-tech means of tapping in to what's going on. Things like feedback from your sales and customer service people. If you've been briefing them and keeping them up to date on the content aspects of your marketing, then they'll be motivated to tell you how well it's working at the coal face. This type of anecdotal feedback can be hugely valuable as you'll get a sense of how useful certain content is in supporting and even improving the sales process, whether that's in initial conversations or helping to close the sale by acting on those 'conviction' and 'action' triggers.

- **Social listening:** Whilst your analytics tools are looking at behaviour, the detail of what people are saying on social platforms is also important and, just like insights from sales, can tell you a lot about what people think about your content, how they are using it, and how useful or entertaining they find it. So keep on top of what comments people are adding when they share on social media and in response to blog posts. This is also your chance to get involved in and encourage those conversations.

- **Direct outreach:** You can also get feedback on your content by simply asking those people consuming it. You may already be running surveys with your customer and opt-in subscriber lists for brand, product or campaign awareness or recall, so think about adapting those to include interaction and engagement with specific content. If your content is a course, book or white paper, then you can also weave a specific survey into your ongoing keep in touch activity to test interest, usefulness, what they liked or disliked most about it, and gather ideas for product or topic development.
- **Take a composite view:** There are many different ways to monitor and measure content performance using a variety of tools and techniques. There's no one solution that will do everything, so you'll be pulling various measures together from different sources.

How to report your results

Using the approach and tools above, you can build aggregated pictures for groups of content items or specific channels and give different people the evaluation view they require. For example, your management team is likely to only be interested in total sales or cost impact this month while your implementers will want a much more granular analysis. Your researchers, writers, designers, producers, channel managers, social media and email experts will want to see how well their specialist area is performing and if there are clues as to how they can improve.

For management reporting, agree relevant key performance indicators (KPIs) and present your evidence. One way to do this is to develop a scorecard or at-a-glance report, tailored for each area if necessary (like CEO, finance or sales), to show how your content marketing strategy is contributing to overall or annual business objectives and goals over time.

You may need to remind people about the long-term nature of a content marketing approach. Although we've just looked at the measurement of a single piece of content, real momentum and therefore a true sense of how successful the approach is proving to be only comes over time – when you've got a long enough track record to refer to. This is quite different to deploying a short term sales tactic or a campaign for something like a product launch.

Over the course of 12 months and beyond, you can start to see the impact of your content marketing on areas such as brand awareness and changes in customer perceptions or attitude to your brand. And be able at least to start to assess the incremental benefit and impact of using content in place of or in addition to whatever you were using before.

Testing and experimenting

One of the great benefits when you have part if not all of your content marketing taking place online is the ability to test different techniques and versions of your content to see what works best.

- Did this headline get more clicks or shares than this one?
- Did video convert more than straight text on this landing page?
- Did the placement of the call-to-action button work better on the right than on the left of the page?
- Did version A of the landing page convert more sign ups than version B?
- Did the page optimized for keyword phrase A deliver more traffic than the one optimized for keyword phrase B?

And so on. This is known as split testing or, not surprisingly, A/B testing. This experimentation is essential to improving your performance over time. While it would be silly to try and test everything, you may have one or two aspects that you want to improve – aspects that have the potential to make a significant difference.

- This could be finding the tone and style that's a perfect match for your audience or for a specific persona. Testing could include different writing styles, language and blog post lengths, different ways of presenting information (how to posts, Q&As, interviews), different media formats, right down to different styles and length of headline.

- Or it could be honing the effectiveness of landing pages as a lead conversion tool – design, layout, writing style, content length, text vs video.

With an ongoing programme of testing and evaluation, you're improving your performance over time and making gradual improvements to your content marketing process and the platforms, techniques and activities that make up that process. It also helps you to manage your budget and phase investment – based on something more substantial than pure guesswork. Which bring us to ...

Return on investment

Traditionally a tricky area for most marketers, return on investment (ROI) calculations are at least made easier with content marketing when you're able to measure the results of your efforts in the way we've discussed above. The other dimension you need of course is to understand what each part of your content marketing process costs you. For anyone with budget responsibility this is an important dimension to consider.

Creating content is resource heavy. Whether you have to manage an existing budget or make the case for new funds, you are at some point going to have to make choices. You have to balance how well a particular content activity is performing in terms of meeting audience and business goals with how much it's costing you and therefore the return you're getting on that investment.

To calculate ROI you need to:

1 Track what content is delivering in the sales funnel and put a monetary value to it. This could be actual sales or the value of a specific set of leads or other conversions. You'll need to work with your sales team to understand what value they assign to leads.
2 Work out what that content cost you.
3 Calculate ROI as (A – B) / B

So, if you conclude that a content-based initiative has generated £2000 and creating, producing and distributing the content has cost you £500, then your ROI is 3 or 300%.

The other side of the coin is how much content marketing is saving you. In deploying content are you making less use of something else? Paid advertising, sponsorship, direct mail, print, and perhaps even direct sales or customer service time?

If you've been used to calculating marketing ROI before adopting a content marketing approach, you can also compare the incremental ROI of content vs whatever you were doing before.

Understanding your costs will also help you to manage your resources more efficiently – especially when deciding to use in-house or external resources. For example, would using a freelance designer or writer be more cost effective than assigning a task to one of your own team or doing it yourself? You have to take into account not just the relative per hour per head cost, but also the cost of any additional training (in-house) or support or supervision (outsource) that may be required. Can you maintain quality or achieve better quality at lower cost by outsourcing and therefore make better use of your budget?

Summary

We've wrapped up our week with a look at content marketing measurement and evaluation. Although it happens at the end of the process, planning what you measure and why must always be done at the start – when you are developing strategy, setting goals, and doing your planning.

It's important to measure things that are meaningful – focusing on effectiveness, impact and outcomes, not just numbers for the sake of numbers.

We looked at:

- What we mean by meaningful measurement, and looked at a simple example
- The measurement methods and tools available to us – online analytics as well as some traditional low-tech options
- How to report results
- Why testing and experimenting is a good idea
- How to develop a return on investment calculation

Whether you are new to marketing or a more seasoned professional picking up content marketing for the first time, don't

SUNDAY
MONDAY
TUESDAY
WEDNESDAY
THURSDAY
FRIDAY
SATURDAY

neglect these aspects of measurement and evaluation because they will enable you to continuously improve your content marketing over time – always remember you are playing the long game.

Fact-check

1. When should you plan how to measure your content?
a) Once you've finished creating and distributing it ❑
b) About a year after you've developed your strategy ❑
c) Right at the start of your content marketing planning ❑
d) Whenever you can fit it in ❑

2. What do we mean by a 'meaningful' measurement?
a) One that gives you the biggest or highest number possible ❑
b) A metric that is a true indicator of what you want to measure ❑
c) One that impresses the Board ❑
d) One that's easy to explain ❑

3. How does an individual item of content relate to your content marketing goals?
a) They're not related at all ❑
b) In a very loose way in the sense that your content sometimes helps generate sales leads ❑
c) They're only connected when you try and match them up at the end of the year ❑
d) Each item of content should directly link to or impact at least one goal ❑

4. When it comes to measurement, a good starting point is:
a) To make sure you put the measurement tools you already have to best use ❑
b) To go out and buy this month's most talked about social media tool ❑
c) To take a quick look at the web stats your IT department issues once a month ❑
d) To wait until your boss asks you a question about how your content is performing ❑

5. Can Google Analytics measure specific website conversions?
a) Yes, you can measure how often people take certain actions on your website ❑
b) No, it only shows numbers of visitors and which pages are read the most ❑
c) Only if you have an e-commerce website ❑
d) Only if someone actually buys something ❑

6. When should you investigate using an automated sales and marketing system?
a) As soon as possible as it'll mean less work for you ❏
b) When the sales director says it's time for you to get one ❏
c) Once you fully understand your marketing process and can choose the right technology to support it ❏
d) When your marketing communications manager resigns ❏

7. Are there additional ways to measure content effectiveness other than web-based systems?
a) No, measurement always takes place online ❏
b) It depends on what products or services you sell ❏
c) Yes, insights from sales people on what customers think about and do with your content can be hugely valuable ❏
d) No, because we only publish our content on our website ❏

8. How can you best report your evaluation results?
a) Write the longest report possible every month as that will impress people ❏
b) Simply distribute a standard Google Analytics report ❏
c) Do nothing – no one will read a report anyway ❏
d) Compile an at-a-glance snapshot for different groups, tailored to show the KPIs they are most interested in ❏

9. What's the benefit of split testing?
a) It gives your team something to do on Fridays ❏
b) It allows you to find out what works best and improve your content performance over time ❏
c) There is no benefit, guessing works just as well ❏
d) It keeps you busy and gives you a good excuse to avoid unnecessary meetings ❏

10. To calculate return on investment you need to know
a) How many website visitors you had this year ❏
b) The monetary value of what your content delivers in the sales funnel and the cost of creating that content ❏
c) How often people shared your content on social media last month ❏
d) Whether your boss is recommending you for a bonus this year ❏

7 × 7

1 Seven useful ways of thinking

Content marketing success is often not so much about what you do as how you go about it, especially the way you think about and approach it.

- Put yourself in your customer's shoes – see and understand the world through their lens.
- Look at a topic from different angles – different perspectives spark different ideas. Get up and move around – both physically and mentally.
- Find a way to the heart of your topic – the main point, the real story, the pot of gold.
- Connect the dots – think in a joined-up way about everything from strategy to execution.
- Adopt an analytical approach – test, observe, and interpret the results to find out what works for you.
- Seek to learn – unleash your curiosity. Keep asking yourself how you can improve and keep on top of emerging trends.
- Learn to think in stories – weave a compelling and honest tale to captivate your audience.

2 Seven in-demand skills

As marketing evolves and more businesses and organizations take more of a content marketing approach, certain skills are much in demand.

- Good writing skills – being able to write well is key not just to creating compelling content but also to brief others in your content team and communicate more widely across your organization.
- Organizational skills – being well organized is essential for keeping the content marketing process running smoothly.

- Understanding what makes content sharable – what it takes to get it picked up and shared across different networks and communities.
- Having an eye for detail – whether that's working with design or words or processes.
- Being able to manage projects and people appropriately, knowing the best techniques to use, when.
- Financial understanding – knowing how to make a business case for content management, setting and making the most of your budget as well as calculating ROI.
- Understanding the psychology of the buyer and learning what the evolving field of neuroscience can contribute to the field of marketing.

3 Seven critical job roles

Content marketing combines traditional marketing roles with those found in publishing, so there are new opportunities to be had inside many of today's evolving marketing departments.

- Researcher – investigating and researching content ideas, conducting interviews and running focus group sessions with audience groups to uncover hot topics.
- Writer – using journalistic skills to turn content ideas into well-crafted, compelling written content.
- Visual content creator – working with images, graphics, and film to create appealing visual content with impact.
- Editor – keeping an eye on consistency of tone, style and quality across all content items and ensuring the desired brand story evolves and is successfully maintained.
- Social media communicator – working with content across social media channels to listen, engage and respond, keeping the conversations going.
- Analyst – using technology and common sense to measure content performance, turn data into actionable information and communicate the results.
- Content team leader – responsible for the process as a whole, keeping the team motivated and on track and

ensuring all the necessary tools and resources are in place and working effectively.

4 Seven key budget considerations

When you consider your content marketing budget, you may first think of salaries and if you will need more people. Here are some of the other key aspects to think about.

- Visual and audio content production – the tools to produce images, graphics, podcasts and video, including studio time and specialist editing.
- Software, systems and tools – to handle monitoring, analysis and management of processes like email marketing right up to a fully formed automated sales and marketing system.
- Website development – to ensure your website is fit for purpose as a publishing and marketing platform and can be easily updated by your content team.
- Paid advertising and sponsorship – for when you need to bring in a little paid help to get your content launched and out there.
- Optimization – specialist support to keep on top of keyword phrase development and spot opportunities, especially if you are a niche player.
- People – recognize the true investment required to hire people with the right skills, whether in-house or through outsourcing.
- Training and networking – no one knows it all and the best content marketers need to hone their skills and keep up to date, whether through formal training, learning from their peers or attending events.

5 Seven common myths

Content marketing is growing but there are still some misconceptions out there – although of course *you* now know better!

- Content marketing doesn't cost you anything. You need resources and a budget just as for any other marketing strategy. In addition content marketing is resource heavy – just look at all that time, commitment and skill required.
- Create content and people will come. Getting your content noticed, picked up and shared does not happen by magic. Distributing and promoting it is as important as creating it.
- Anyone can write. Anyone can write something, but not everyone can write compelling content and all the best writers write a lot and continuously strive to improve their skills.
- It's all about rapid content creation – just turn on the mic or camera and press 'go'. You can get away with this only if you're working with a charismatic, media savvy person. Many of your content sources are not natural performers, so need handling accordingly.
- It's all about quantity. Volume of content is not as important as quality. Whilst you need to understand how much content you need to publish to gain 'traction', quality must always come first.
- It only happens online. Content can be published and consumed anywhere. Some of the most successful initiatives integrate content across online, offline and in-person channels.
- Optimization is just for search engines. Search engines are just tools that people use to find things, so always write for your audience first and foremost.

6 Seven inspiring quotes

Content marketing can be a little challenging at times, so here are a few helpful hints.

- 'Marketing is no longer about the stuff that you make but about the stories you tell.' Seth Godin
- 'Traditional marketing and advertising is telling the world you're a rock star. Content Marketing is showing the world that you are one.' Robert Rose, Chief Strategy Officer, Content Marketing Institute